AF117727

GLIMPSES OF Jean

The story of Jean Zuvela-Doda
Lady of the Lime Kilns

Edited by Jenny Kroonstuiver

This is an IndieMosh book

brought to you by MoshPit Publishing
an imprint of Mosher's Business Support Pty Ltd

PO Box 147
Hazelbrook NSW 2779

indiemosh.com.au

Copyright © Jenny Kroonstuiver 2020

The moral right of the author has been asserted in accordance with the Copyright Amendment (Moral Rights) Act 2000.

All rights reserved. Except as permitted under the Australian Copyright Act 1968 (for example, fair dealing for the purposes of study, research, criticism or review) no part of this publication may be reproduced, stored in a retrieval system, or transmitted in any form or by any means, electronic, mechanical, photocopying, recording or otherwise, without the written permission of the publisher.

 A catalogue record for this work is available from the National Library of Australia

https://www.nla.gov.au/collections

Title:	Glimpses of Jean
Subtitle:	The story of Jean Zuvela-Doda
Author:	Kroonstuiver, Jenny
ISBNs:	978-1-922368-89-8 (paperback)
Subjects:	BIOGRAPHY & AUTOBIOGRAPHY / General; Women; Historical; HISTORY / Oceania

This work depicts actual events in the life of its subject Jean Zuvela as truthfully as recollection permits and/or can be verified by research. Occasionally, dialogue consistent with the character or nature of the person speaking has been supplemented. All persons within are actual individuals; there are no composite characters. The names of some individuals have been changed to respect their privacy.

Cover concept by Jenny Kroonstuiver

Cover design and layout by Ally Mosher at allymosher.com

Cover and internal images from Jenny Kroonstuiver's personal archive

Acknowledgments

This book could not have been written without the foresight of Norma King, who taped Jean Zuvela's story, and then had the confidence in me to hand over the tapes. I am extremely grateful for not only her vote of confidence, but her guidance, patience and advice in preparing the book.

Mary Seuter, Jean's sister, similarly, assisted greatly with photographs, her own stories, and infinite patience as what was originally a one-year project stretched into several. I thank Mary and her family for allowing me to write this story.

To all the other contributors, Heather Crombie, my parents, Ruth and Eric Swann and all of those who assisted with the research, I am extremely grateful.

To my own family, for their advice, encouragement and patience – thank you. I know it has taken over fifteen years to finally bring this book to print but here it is, at last.

Jenny Kroonstuiver 2020

Foreword

I first met Jean Zuvela in 1963. I was eight years old and my father had taken on the job of establishing a huge sheep station, Kanandah, on the Nullarbor Plain, in Western Australia. At that time, Aunty Jean, as she soon became known, was living with her husband, Mark Zuvela, in the small Yugoslav community at the Lime Kilns on the 913 mile peg of the Trans Australian Railway.

My earliest memories of Aunty Jean's home are of a small dwelling built from railway sleepers, corrugated iron sheets and hessian bags, and of pine furniture built from fruit boxes. I remember the kitchen best, a myriad of friendly smells, cups of tea, and never-ending treats. It was here that we, as children, were called 'shrimp' and 'sausage'; ate magnificent roast dinners and watched with fascination the never-ending supply of beer bottles.

The Lime Kilns were a child's paradise. Mark was a man of mystery with three fingers missing – he sagely warned us that that would happen to us too, if we sucked our fingers. There were birds that talked, a three-legged dog, a bull that ate soap, a wedge-tail eagle with a rope on its leg, a baby camel and goats. It was a place where parental authority was gently overruled.

Not only did Aunty Jean have an exceptional life spanning two cultures, but her extraordinary memory provided a rich tapestry of life experiences.

She was an amazing conversationalist. Her dialogue resembled a spider web: in recalling a single incident she interwove the re-telling with a hundred anecdotes of family genealogies and interlinked recollections, always returning eventually to the original point, but in the meantime treating the listener to a fascinating maze of memories. She barely drew breath – conversations with Aunty Jean were one-sided and lengthy, but never regretted, because to listen was a little like having a film described, complete with all the scenery, secondary images and symbolism.

It was when my own daughter, Heidi, chose 'Aunty Jean – a Kalgoorlie Pioneer' as a subject in a public speaking competition that I suddenly realised that this extraordinary life needed to be recorded.

In 1996 it was time to write. Aunty Jean was growing increasingly frail and I wanted this to be her story, not mine. I shall always regret not having started then and there, but other responsibilities took over and the writing was delayed. It was not until after Aunty Jean's death, that I finally commenced writing.

Shortly before Aunty Jean died, Norma King took the time to tape Aunty Jean's stories, and willingly handed them over to me to commit to paper. Aunty Jean thus has told her own story, and I have simply provided the editing to translate the spoken word to the written.

There are so many gaps. Aunty Jean herself was selective in her telling. To have known Jean Zuvela during her life is to understand that no book could truly cover her depth of character or wealth of experiences, hence the title – *Glimpses of Jean*.

Jean Strika, aged about 13

Contents

Acknowledgments v

Foreword vi

Chapter 1: Gwalia to Fremantle 1

Chapter 2: Move to the Nullarbor 19

Chapter 3: Life on the Kilns 38

Chapter 4: People of the Kilns 50

Chapter 5: The Kilns at Work 58

Chapter 6: Language and Names 62

Chapter 7: Friends, visitors and neighbours....................... 66

Chapter 8: After Work 81

Chapter 9: The Kilns close 88

Eulogy for Jean: By Eric Swann 97

About the Author 101

Chapter 1
Gwalia to Fremantle

Restored miner's cottage, Gwalia 1996

...sent away to a strange country to a woman that couldn't speak her language...

My mother's name was Tomasina Kazea. She was born on an island called Zlarin off the Dalmatian coast of Yugoslavia and her Uncle, Matt Kazea, arranged for her to be brought out from Yugoslavia ... she said she had her eleventh birthday when she was passing through the Red Sea. I couldn't say what ship she came on. Uncle had taken his wife over to see where her people came from in Ireland, and then over to France for the Paris exhibition (in 1900), then to Venice and to Germany, because one of his wife's sisters had married a German chap, and they went up to Tipplets, I think it is, in Germany.

Then Uncle called into his birthplace, Zlarin, and went to see his sister-in-law who was my Grandma. (There were two brothers that I know of, Matt Kazea and Andrew Kazea. Andrew Kazea was my Mum's father.) They stayed with her for a while ... she only had my mother, that's all, because her husband, he was a stoker on ships. Where my mother comes from, most of the people were captains or lawyers or doctors or worked on sailing ships in those days. But Andrew Kazea, my mother's father, was a stoker – it must have been a steamship – and they used to knock off work, because it was hot, and they'd come up and lay on deck, and he got pneumonia and it turned into consumption and he died with that. He died when she was 11 months or 11 weeks old – 11 something, only a baby.

She was an only child like I was for a while. And her Uncle and Auntie talked it over with my Grandma about bringing Mum over here to give her a better chance. Well, they came back home and they must have written and Grandma agreed to send the daughter out here. So another chap, by the name of Sam Ljuba, was coming out to Fremantle and he brought Mum right to Matt Kazea – to her own Uncle there.

She told me later that this Auntie and Uncle wanted to adopt me when I was a baby, but she said "I wouldn't do what my Mother done to me … sent me to strange people in another country". I would have still been here, but she was sent away to a strange country to a woman that couldn't speak her language, and so she said when Auntie and Uncle wanted to adopt me she said no. Mum had married again when I was two years old, but she said: "No way".

When she came out here she arrived in Fremantle and I believe they stayed there for a while because she told me she went to North Fremantle School. Then they left there and came up and lived in Piesse Street in Boulder for a while and she went to that school … I suppose it would be Boulder Central. Then they went up to Gwalia and Uncle worked on the mines, and she went to school in Gwalia and stayed there and got married there aged eighteen years and four months.

Mum went to school up there, and she said it was really hard because she couldn't speak to Aunty and Aunty couldn't speak to her. She could only speak to her Uncle because she couldn't speak English. They reared her from 11 years old – they never had any children themselves.

Mum married when she was 18 years and 4 months old. The chap she came out with, Sam Ljuba, well she married his brother – who was my father. My mother got married in 1907 in Gwalia. Her husband's name was Fortunata Ljuba, but everybody called him Frank. Then he got killed when I was five months old, in October 1909. Killed in an underground skip accident. Then afterwards when everything was all finalised, they left.

My brother took me up to Leonora years later. I'd love to have gone to Gwalia when it was still a thriving place, but it was a ghost town when we went – and it's not so good – but my husband would never bother to go up there. Anyway I got up and found my father's grave. It was still in good condition – the cross was still there and it wasn't bowled over; of the five domes there was only one of them broken. The rest were as good as gold after all those years. But there was a lot of young people died or got killed on the mines buried there at Gwalia. We went to look at that museum there, and I was looking through the Catholic register, and I found the registration of my father's death.

In that time while she was married, Mum brought her mother out from Yugoslavia and she came up to Gwalia and stayed with Mum for six months but she didn't like it. She wanted to go home even though all she had was that daughter – she had never married again. I don't know what she done in the old country ... nobody ever told me, and I don't know much of my side of the family at all. I know more about my step-father's family than I do my own. And, anyway, in the finish, Mum sent her home because she didn't like it out here ... so she sent her back to the Old Country.

Mum said there were a lot of Italian ladies in Gwalia then, but I never heard her mention a lot of Slav. Some Slav men, but more Italians I think than Slavs. My step-father was up there and one chap who was my Godfather, but he left. Then another chap we knew, Peter Pekich, he must have worked on the mines. He left too, and the next time I saw him was when I was living with my Auntie and Uncle in Fremantle, when they were living in the wine saloon.

I've heard Mum speak of Patronis in Gwalia – the boarding house. I was looking at some photos, and I said to the lady who was at the museum: "That name is familiar. I've heard my mother and Auntie talk about them." And people by the name of Softley – I've heard Mum mention them too. I went down to Perth on the train one day and met another old chap who lives up (I think) in Hanbury Street – his name was Softley – he used to be shoeing horses and things there. Well, his mother – he was trying to say some name – I mentioned the name Scribb – and he said "Oh yes, I know Auntie Scribb" and he said there was another – "Kizzy" – and I said, "You mean Kazea?" He said "Yes", and apparently his mother and my mother's Auntie were cousins, and his mother lived in Trafalgar and my mother's Aunty used to go to Trafalgar when they lived in Piesse Street in Boulder, to see his mother. I said: "What a little world", because I'd heard my Mum and Auntie Kazea speak about Softleys.

So when Mum and Auntie and Uncle left Gwalia, they went down to Fremantle very close to Collie Street. They had rooms as well there. Mum used to work with Auntie and Uncle and help them in the wine saloon.

I think my Mum, coming out here young and living with an Aussie Aunty, she nearly forgot her own language. But when my father died and Mum went with her Aunty and Uncle in the wine saloon in Fremantle, in those days a lot of Yugoslav blokes used to come and Yugoslav fishermen, and that wine saloon was a boarding house as well – had rooms like a hotel. A lot of fishermen used to come there, and a lot of Slav sailors from Slav boats who knew that Uncle was a Slav, would go there because they could speak their own language, and it came back to my Mum quite easily.

Then she met my stepfather when I was about two years old, but they used to go to school together in the old country. My step-father was about three years older than Mum – he came out here when he was only 16 – I don't know what year that was. He used to be up in Gwalia too, working on the mines. Mum met him again when I was two years old. Then they married and I think Mum told me that they went up to Hines Hill. His name was Fortunata Strika, and he was called Frank Strika.

When they left Hines Hill, they went to Kellerberrin where my eldest brother was born. Then they left there and went down to Fremantle way where my second eldest brother was born. Jack was the first son and the second was called Frank after his father. Then they came back to the Goldfields and Dad worked at Lakeside out on the Woodline there, and then he worked on the mines as well and then another brother was born.

There were seven of us

We kicked around the bush a lot when we were kids, because having a big family, Dad went wherever there was contract work, chopping wood, or clearing or something like that. I started school in Boulder and then I went to Fremantle Catholic School and then to the convent in Kellerberrin, then we went to Hamilton Hill School. When they came down from Boulder we were going to the Hamilton Hill School – my brothers started there and I think the younger brother started out at Spearwood afterwards. We went to Jandakot and Peel Estate as well, and then I left school when I was about thirteen and went to work.

There were seven of us, but I'm the only one from Mum's first husband, because I was born in Gwalia before my father got killed in the Sons of Gwalia mine. There were three brothers and when I was just on 9 years old Mum had twin girls and a year or so after that, no two years after, we had another baby brother.

My name was Ljuba, but everybody called me Strika after my mother married my stepfather. I got on well with him; if I got a hiding I deserved it – the same with the others. He worked on the Lakeside

Woodline– there used to be the Lakeside and the Lakewood and the Kurrawang Woodline. He lived at Lakeside – he worked there and he went to work on the mines when the war broke out.

After Hines Hill we went to live on the Boulder Block, close to the Ivanhoe dump. In those days they used to come around with a tank on a cart and ask how much water we'd want – they'd put the gallons of water in your tank – we had to buy it. Then we shifted from there to King Street where we were living when I started school. It's a long time ago, but when you think back it seems just like yesterday.

They used to put us out on a chair

I started school in Boulder there when I was six. I remember coming home one day from school in Boulder – I started at the Catholic school – I felt crook, my head was aching and my throat was sore. Mum got the doctor next day and I had diphtheria and had to go to the isolation ward – in those days they had a horse-drawn ambulance.

I was put in the isolation ward in the hospital, but they've pulled it down now – I was there for five weeks. There were a lot of kiddies in that ward and another child came in, and I think she only had diphtheria, but there was no other spare bed, and she was put at the foot of the bed … my bed. And there was another older lady. Old? To me she was old, but now looking back I can see that woman, she had long dark hair and she might have been only in her twenties. But to me then she was an old woman, because I was only a kid of six years old. She was in that isolation ward, in bed.

I was over there for about five weeks before I went home. When we got better, they used to put us out on a chair, wrap us around and sit us on the front of that place, and my mother used to come up. I can visualise the picket fence, and Mum used to push the pram up there. She never used to come inside and she only used to talk to me from the gateway in the picket fence because being an isolated ward there, she could only sing out to me. It was a picket fence coming up to the verandah, at the front part of the isolation ward and from there she could talk; that's the only time I ever saw Mum.

After five weeks in there my stepfather came and picked me up and took me home and I was home for a week there and then I went to school for about one week. The nuns never put me to sit with the kids where I was before – they put me over to one side to sit on a box at a little table by myself. I felt awful, stuck away by myself as if I had leprosy or something. I was a week there, and Mum saw I didn't seem to be picking up, so when her brother-in-law was going to Perth Mum sent me down with him to her Aunty – she thought a break down near the sea would do me good.

I went down to my mother's Aunty for about two years and never came back to Kalgoorlie until 1933. I had my eighth birthday at Aunty and Uncle's in Spearwood where they had a vineyard and I lived with them until Mum and Dad came down from Kalgoorlie.

When they came down they stayed for a while with Aunty and Uncle in Fremantle, then we all went up to Kellerberrin, out on a wheat farm. Dad and another fellow used to have the wheat farm before he went to Gwalia, but they sold it when Dad got married to Mum and came up to the Goldfields.

Mum had twin daughters on the farm – Auntie came up and delivered them as well. I was eight years old and eight months when they were born, but I'd gone to the convent. They'd sent me to the convent in Kellerberrin, when the Catholic convent first opened up. I had more to do with my brothers and sisters later, after we left Kellerberrin and came back down to Fremantle, then I had more to do with them. There was so much difference between me and my sisters – my brothers were closer.

At the end of the year – I know I had my ninth birthday in the convent – at the end of the year I had two brothers ready for school and they couldn't afford to have three of us in Kellerberrin and so Dad left there and went back to Fremantle, and from there we went to the Beaconsfield State School for a while, and then to Jandakot – we walked about three and a half miles to school there. Then back into Fremantle and we went to Beaconsfield Sate School again.

Eva died in Mum's arms...

We were living in South Fremantle when my sister, one of the twins, died ... she got croup and diphtheria. She was two years and eleven months old. Then the baby brother who would have been a year old in the April, he died on the 19th ... sixteen days after my sister died. One on the 3rd December and one on the 19 December. Vickie was the little boy who died ... Eva was the name of the little girl who died.

We were all sick, I had got the measles, the second oldest brother, Frank, had the measles, Jack got the measles and then it turned to bronchitis and pneumonia, and third brother, Tom, he'd got the measles and whooping cough. The oldest brother, Jack, he had measles first, but then he got a chill and got bronchitis and pneumonia, and he was sent to the isolation ward. We went up to see him when he was shifted into the ordinary ward. He said to Mum, "Where's Vickie? You haven't brought Vickie up". Mum's Auntie was there and she said... "Oh no, he's dead", and Jack never said another word, he never spoke or said goodbye when we left. It was such a shock to him. He was only eight years old. He already knew that Eva had died ... she had died before he went to hospital.

The little girl, Eva, had died in Mum's arms in Dr Gibson's motorcar going to hospital. The little boy died in the hospital. Mum was the only one that never got sick – even Dad got ill afterwards. Mum sent one of the next door neighbour's sons ... Dad worked for people called Mortimer who had quarries out at Spearwood way ... and they sent Bobby Collins out on the bike to tell Dad to come home because Eva had died. And this was in the dinner hour, and her Uncle Matt Kazea was working at the smelters at South Fremantle and poor old Uncle didn't know what to do and he just got up and went away back to work. Mum told me to get dressed and go into town and get Auntie ... her Uncle's wife, and she came out.

Well it was an awful hot summer then. This happened in December ... when all of us were sick. When the baby died, I was still getting over the measles and when Mum came from the hospital home I was in bed. She just came and said ... she said that she'd told the nurse there ... she said that he doesn't look as good as what he did. He could go anytime.

When the Health Inspector came around they found that it was diphtheria in the house and they found out that the third oldest brother was the carrier of the diphtheria. We were living right at South Fremantle, at the terminus there ... we had a house there, and then they sold it and we went and lived at Spearwood.

We went out to Peel Estate. Mum used to make beautiful homemade bread when we lived on Peel Estate, and she used to bake bread in a camp oven. We had three tents there, one was our bedroom for the kids, that one was made out of wheat bags ... we sewed them up. Dad made a tent out of the bags, and the kitchen, it was in between, and the other was a ten by twelve or twelve by fourteen tent, and that was Mum and Dad's bedroom. They had a double bed, and a cot for the young sister, Eva's twin. I was twelve and she was three, and she used to sleep in the cot. Two brothers were in the double bed in the other big tent, and the older brother and I had a single bed each there.

In the winter months when it was cold, so Mum didn't have to get out of bed, they made a wagga ... sewed the bags up with a bit of rope on the end, and Mum used to tie it down ... each end like that, so that the blankets wouldn't fall off. I would have been twelve or thirteen, then the older brother would have been ten and the next brother nine and the other one was seven and they used to wriggle around, and so the clothes wouldn't fall off, Mum used to tie the wagga in the winter.

I broke a chamber pot one day

I left school when I was about thirteen and a half and went to work ... I worked in Fremantle, where the Town Hall is in Fremantle. Well they had the Town Hall Bedrooms upstairs there, and I used to work for a Miss White. There were three sisters, Norma, Delia and Peg, and two brothers, Jim and Mick ... Irish people, they had the bedrooms.

It was called the Town Hall Bedrooms, but there was a laneway between the Town Hall and these bedrooms and there were shops. The lady I worked for ... her sister Norma was a dressmaker and done millinery work there as well. She used to sell these hats, make them and was a dressmaker. She had a room in the bedrooms that her sister used to look after, and their sister Peg and Jim used to help as well, and then I came along and used to help her and got ten shillings a week. I started work at half past seven until I'd finished. I lived again with my mother's Auntie. Auntie had like a bed-sitting room in this little house and you had to go downstairs to go into the kitchen. I had a three-quarter bed and Auntie did as well. She was only on the pension in those days.

I'll never forget that first day's work as long as I live. It was a Monday, washing day and I can remember those sheets. I had to rinse them and blue them there sixty-five sheets. They didn't have a mangle. And when I came home I came inside and threw myself on the bed and said "Oh Auntie, I'm tired". I'll never forget that day's work, and all for ten shillings a week. Gee I was tired.

Breakfast I had at home, and I got my lunch there and then you finished work of an evening. The lady done the washing but I done the rinsing and blueing of the darn things, and hung them on the line. She done the actual dirty work, the rubbing and the washing ... and then I'd help through the rest of the day, help to make the beds with her sister Peg. We used to sweep the floors. In those days, there was one chap, Mr O'Neill, he was a tramways inspector and he never married, and he had lino there, and a girl they had had before had put the dirt under the lino, and he saw that and got the lady to take the lino off the floor so they just had those pine boards. You never had much cleaning gear, you only had the scrubbing brush and the cloth, and you had to get down and scrub the pine boards. But most of the others had lino.

They nearly always had somebody living there. Some were there for quite a while ... just lived, rented a room and lived there and worked as well. It wasn't an eating place at all, there was only one old man and he was the only one that ever ate there. I don't know whether he was a friend, or what, but he was there for a long, long while.

But as I say there were three sisters ... one sister was in business and the other two used to run the place with the brother, Jim. Those days, you know you didn't have the bathrooms and toilets and everything. The toilets were downstairs, but you had the chamber and the basin, the wash-basin. I didn't have to empty the chambers, the boss's brother he used to empty all that out ... the slops. And the jug, you always topped that up with fresh water the next day, for the person that's got the room.

I broke a chamber one day, one of those pots. By that time I'd turned fourteen and there was a shop down towards where the Fremantle station was and I had to go down there and buy one. I had to pay for it myself, because I had broken it, and a boy about my age came along to ask me what I wanted, and I looked everywhere but in his face to tell him I wanted a chamber. I felt that embarrassed. I've never bought one since, that was the only time … it was one of those porcelain ones. Two and sixpence it was out of my ten shillings a week.

But in those days you could get a lot in a way for ten shillings. I gave Auntie money because I lived at her place and other meals I had there. I had to go to Church too, every Sunday – the ladies were very strict Catholics. I used to work every day, Sundays and all, but I had to go to Church first, so it didn't matter if I started later. It was mass at half-past seven, but one day I missed it and I thought My God, if they ask me what did the Priest say … what Priest said mass I wouldn't know. Then they tried to get me to join the – I think it was called the Children of Mary – and I went up to a meeting there, but I'm afraid, I don't know, I had nobody, was just by myself, and I didn't know anybody else there. I went that once and I didn't go any more. I did go to Church just the same every Sunday and Dad used to make us go to Church – "While you're under my roof, you'll go every Sunday to mass. When you leave then you can please yourself," he would say.

We had mostly vegetables

Mum and Dad were living at Peel Estate then. I was thirteen years and seven months. I just got that job and stayed with Auntie, and worked all the time after that.

I worked there for eleven months then left and went to work for other people out near the Newmarket Hotel, for Mr and Mrs Atkinson.

He used to be the manager and the shareholder of Anchorage Butchers. I went there to look after the children. When I was younger, I used to go to school with some of their kiddies and some of their nieces and nephews at Beaconsfield State School. I worked there for about eight or nine months until my stepfather got a vegetable garden in Spearwood and then I stopped work and worked in the garden with my mother and stepfather. We had mostly vegetables, a few vines, but we never sold any grapes, just vegies and that's where he got electrocuted there in a well. At that time I was eighteen.

We had two wells on the property, the one that was more near to the main road, the sand had been falling all the time and so they had another well, and it was on a slant. One was sixty or sixty-five feet deep, and that other was about seventy-five feet deep and it was higher ground and it was a bit rocky around the bottom as well. Then they built a drive inside where the motor was put and to clean it all out ... you couldn't work while the engine was going because of the belt that drove the motor. The two older brothers, Jack and Frank were there, they had a windlass there to pull up the dirt from the bottom of the drive they were cleaning out but apparently there must have been a leakage of electricity there. Anyway, the second eldest brother was down the well with his father, and my father sent him up because when they were turning the windlass around the bucket would sway and Frank, he'd keep the rope kind of pushed away the bucket would only come up so far and he couldn't get it to shift out. He sang out to Dad that the bucket won't come up, but it'd go down like, so he tried again and it came again and he said: "It's still stuck". Apparently it was deep down and must have swayed and was catching under a ledge somewhere. Then my father must have gone to swing the bucket out and apparently he got electrocuted just touching that.

They only heard him sing out "Oh God!" twice and no more. They couldn't go down the well – it kind of come all like smoke or something in it. We went over to the next door neighbour – people by the name of Prelonga, and Mum asked him if he would go down. He said: "ask me anything Mrs Strika, but don't ask me to go down the well." So we went to another chap next door – to this Italian fellow by the name of Tom Dusovich, and he came along and got an axe and cut and cut until he cut through a half-inch pipe where the electric light wires went down. The pipe didn't go all the way down and some of the wires were just down the side of the wall bare, and they must have worn or something and there was a leakage of electricity. There was no motor going because you couldn't work there, so he thought the best thing he could do was get the axe and cut right through the pipe.

That happened around five o'clock and they couldn't get down into the well because it got full of fumes. Around nine o'clock they brought the body up. Mr Dusovich and another young chap, he was only a boy of fifteen there and he helped to bring Dad out. But we never saw him any more and the undertaker said for Mum just to remember him as he was. Apparently I think he got burnt on the face. The same undertaker, Mr Sempkin, that buried my father in Gwalia, he was down in Fremantle and he buried the second husband too.

Honestly, I don't know how Mum managed

Mum wasn't twenty when she lost the first husband ... and when she lost the second she was 38 and he was 41. We kept on in the gardens for a little while, but then we left it too because the oldest brother, Jack, got a complaint about a bad hip and he got tuberculosis of the hip. The younger brother, Tom, left school straight after; he refused to go back to school, and he went to work for people by the name of Mair-Brindles.

My brother Frank, he was the only one left there, and my sister who went to High School.

Jack couldn't go to work, he ended up in hospital, he had a big cyst as well there and they cut that out and said it would be about a week in Fremantle Hospital but he was there for about five weeks. Then it broke out further up and he was about nineteen weeks in the Perth Hospital there.

Honestly I don't know how Mum managed ... I couldn't tell you. I went and got a job. Good friends in Spearwood collected money once there and I remember Mr Mair coming across, they had a big farm – Mair and Brindles – and they used to give Mum the money. Then Frank left school when he was fifteen, and he went and worked for them too and he got twenty-five shillings a week and he used to give that to Mum. At seventeen years of age he used to get five shillings to go out Saturday night, the bus fare into town and the pictures there. Frank and Tom used to give it all to Mum, and then I went and got a job as well, and so that left only the younger sister mostly, and the other brother was more in hospital than he was out of it and he got a pension then when he was seventeen.

Mum stayed at Spearwood at that place for as long as she could, and then the bank took it over because she wasn't all paid off and the bank people let her stay there in the house as caretaker of that property. There was another house on the property, Slav people, and they paid more rent than we did. We used to grow a little bit of stuff for our own purposes, but not to send to market any more. The Slav chap worked on the roads – it was the time of depressions. You worked for the money you got paid like you get the dole today. In those days if there was two in the family you got two days' work – seven shillings they used to get for each person.

After Dad got killed, I got a job back with the Atkinsons, where I looked after the children. I went back there cooking afterwards. It was a private home they had, a big place; he was the managing shareholder of Anchorage Butchers. They had racehorses and all and they had two other girls working for them, they had a cook and another one that did the housework. The place had about twenty rooms. I was eighteen when Dad got killed and I saw where they advertised for a cook and I said to Mum: "Look I'm going down to the Post Office" – I had about a mile to go down – and I rang up and got the job. I think working there before gave me an advantage because they knew me there and it was a live-in job I got for a pound a week and my food. So that was one less out of the family, and then I could give Mum a bit of money too as well. And my two younger brothers were working and they gave her money and helped out.

It was close to this time that Auntie died, too. When I think back, it could have been cancer. Her lungs were all gone and she used to stay with my mother in Spearwood until she got ill. She had a friend, a Mrs McDougall, who ran the Hostel Manly, and she said: "Come up and stay with me for a while". And this Mrs McDougall had a retarded son – he was born crippled, and he couldn't do nothing, couldn't shave himself, bath himself. His mother did everything for him from birth. He was just like a baby in a way but he'd talk to you.

Mrs McDougall said: "Jean, would you come up?" I went up and stayed at Mrs McDougall's at the hostel Manly, and on the weekend I used to go home to Spearwood. I just wasn't working at the time when Auntie died, and she wasn't very long at the Hostel Manly, maybe a couple of weeks, before she died. I used to go up now and then just to help, just to carry the food to Auntie and to look after Auntie most of all. She always used to put her hand on my shoulder – she was a big woman, fifteen or sixteen stone, a shade shorter than me – to go up to the toilet and help her. Then she used to have a pot on the thing, and I used to help do that, because Mrs McDougall had her son to look after, and they had a shop.

It was in the November of 1930 when Auntie died, when Phar Lap won the Melbourne Cup. She was mad on horse racing, and she said, even as sick as she was, that Phar Lap was going to win the Melbourne Cup. When they lived in the wine saloon they used to go to the races and take me when I was a kid of six or seven years old. One day I went up to see her at Mrs McDougall's, and Auntie said: "A man was in my room, Jean".

I said "Who? There couldn't be, Auntie, because there's no one here." I said: "You know you can't walk, and Mr McDougall's up in Kalgoorlie. Who was it?"

She said: "It was Jesus, he was standing at that door".

So whether she thought that or what I don't know. And I went home that weekend and Mrs McDougall rang up and said that Auntie had passed away, and then Mr Sempkin buried her as well. I was twenty when she died. I was closer to Auntie because Auntie was very strict with Mum. I don't know why, whether it because my Mum couldn't speak English or what, but she was hard on Mum and with me she was very soft. If she gave threepence to me, my brothers would only get a penny.

Chapter 2
Move to the Nullarbor

Jean and Mark, pictured with Jean's mother (left)

Keasey Brothers opened the Lime Kilns

That lime out there was 96-98% pure lime, not like the lime that's down around Spearwood, Coogee and East Fremantle way – one bag of that lime from the Nullarbor, you'd have to use 2 or 3 of the bags from Fremantle. The Keasey Bros had kilns down Fremantle way as well, because my stepfather used to work for Keasey Brothers in Spearwood. Then Mr Keasey came up to where the Kilns were going to be built and tried to burn some of the stone and found out just how good it was and then they opened up a kiln there in 1931.

They had three kilns and later on they built another one. Mr Keasey put those kilns in a nice patch there, but as it was they had to go a long way for wood. The railway siding was built eight miles west of where the kilns were built and then later they put a siding closer. It was called Lime Siding.

Well, the fellow who was best man at our wedding – he came from the same village as my husband did in Yugoslavia – he got my husband the job there. Keasey Bros wanted more men there so Ralph wrote down to my husband who came up, then they wanted some more men, and then my husband, (he wasn't my husband then) wrote to me and said would my brother Frank want a job. Frank arrived up there in the year of 1932 on Christmas Day – but they wanted more men, so Frank wrote to our eldest brother Jack who went up there about January of 1933.

I went out there in March of 1933, and by then the chap I later married was already there, and I had two brothers working there. I already had a job with Atkinsons, but when my oldest brother wrote to me and said would I give up my job to housekeep for them and they'd give me the same kind of wages I was getting down there – so I did. My two brothers and the chap I was going to marry, and the chap who turned out to be best man at the wedding – the four of them batched together.

For part of the time I was the only woman there – but mostly they had other Slav women there, and other Aussie women too. They had about twenty-two men. Mrs Keasey was there first, and then a Mrs Hales when I first went up there, and another Yugoslav lady, and myself. Mrs Hales and I went out on the same train in March 1933. Her husband was already out there.

When the men left Spearwood it took them about a week to come up by truck to the Lime Kilns at Naretha on the Trans Line. They came there with nothing, they put tents up and then they made these huts with the bag walls. You know the rusty kerosene tins that were along the line, well they opened these kerosene tins out and flattened them, and all their kitchen part was just covered with these kerosene tins … that was the roof. Of a night-time when you've got no light in the kitchen and you looked up you could see the stars through those holes. And bit-by-bit they got iron and put it over the rest of the roof, but the walls were all made of bag.

Later after I was married I shifted to another place next door to this girl Keasey who used to do the cooking. And what was the kitchen we made into the bedroom, and we made what was the dining area our kitchen and the smaller part, Mark made that into a bedroom. Then he built a verandah thing on with old sleepers, and then the firm got some iron and he made a sort of enclosed verandah and later on put a bit of a porch at the back. It was lined inside with filtercloth. That was my second home.

Afterwards, when we got to manage the place, another house was empty. Like all the other places it was only bag with sleeper floors and proper iron on the roof there. Two rooms were made of iron but inside it was lined with filtercloth and the two other rooms were just filtercloth and bag, and the front verandah … well, that we had enclosed. And so we stayed there until we left.

There were twelve camps that I know of. They weren't all next-door, they were kind of here, there and everywhere. It wasn't made in streets, they were just here and there. The biggest camp would have been about four rooms, just bags and filtercloth and all the bags were sewn together. When the place was opened up in 1931, the boarding house, that was only made with a timber table, with planks down the middle and they made a bench or stool, a long one down each side of it. I used to live up in the camp I first came in, and I done the cooking down there, and I had about ten men to cook for. There were Slavs and English people there then.

When I first went up there, we had nothing, just one of those old Coolgardie stretchers and I put up a bit of sheeting against the bag wall and then some nails in the thing and then I used to hang things on a hanger and I used to hang another bit of sheet over the top to keep the dust from going on the clothes. I had 2 or 3 boxes at the side of the bed to put the lamp on. The stretchers were the wire ones … not cycloney altogether, they had some bits of wood there, and the legs would fold up underneath out of the way if you wanted to. After a time they would get saggy. The mattresses were the kapoky ones … they were alright. When you're young there you sleep on anything.

My first home there was just bag walls

At first we had the kitchen and Mark, the chap that was going to be my husband, my brother and the fellow who was best man at my wedding – they had a bedroom of their own, and they made another bedroom separate for me altogether. My oldest brother lived across the way in another camp with another fellow, but they all ate in the place where my second oldest brother and the chap that was going to be my husband ate.

I never had a safe when I first went there – my husband made me one later, out of some 2x3 and fracture boxes. It was a square safe and the fracture boxes were put on the top with a bit of wood across the middle so that I could lean my plates and put cup things in – that was my kind of kitchenette. My cupboards, where you kept tins – it was mostly tinned stuff there – were those fruit boxes, about the size of kerosene boxes, jarrah ones. Well I used to have, say, four of them put on top of one another – there'd be eight – put them close together and put curtains across and that was my cupboard where I kept all my tinned stuff. I never kept anything in packets; in fact I went around the rubbish heaps – you may not believe that – and where they'd thrown out screw-top jars, I'd save them there.

Today I don't buy much tinned stuff. I might get tinned peaches or something like that but we had to have tinned peas or beans, tinned sausages, wham, bully beef or 'tinned dog' as I call it. Tinned curry and salmon … I'd curry that or make salmon patties. Vegetables you couldn't keep for very long. Potatoes and onions were the main thing. I'd always get 25lb plain flour and 25lb self-raising flour then I always had flour if I ran short of bread; I could make scones or something. I'm no good at making bread. First lot I made, I said to the girl who lived next door: "Have a look at the bread." There was yards of it, and I can remember it was like elastic, it never rose up, it was all just horrible dough. Sometimes we used to get a case of beer and we'd wrap it up in a wet chaff bag, and we'd just take it around wherever there was a cool breeze and used to think that bottle of beer was really beautiful.

We kept company for about five years before we got married. I went out in thirty three and was married in thirty-four.

We came in to Kalgoorlie just after the race riots happened because we had friends out at Boulder ... all we could see out there was the chimney things standing, or old iron bedsteads where they had got burnt. That was the year we went down to get married. Mum had got the banns called out when we got down there. We got married in the first Catholic church that was built in Spearwood. Archbishop Clune was the Archbishop then and Dr Goodie (who was Archbishop after Archbishop Clune died), he'd been in Yugoslavia at a monastery or a church over in the old country and he could speak and read and write Slav. He said the whole mass in the Yugoslav language, and there was one old lady, and she was crying in the Church and she said: "I never thought I'd hear the mass in my tongue again". There were a lot of Yugoslavs there.

The week after that I got married, say that was the Sunday, and the following Saturday 12 May 1934, I was married. The church was called St Jeremy, and now they've built a new Catholic church in Spearwood and they've taken the statue of St Jeremy from the first church they built and put it in the new one.

An English fellow, Mr Berry, he had a butcher's shop; he gave me away at the wedding. And this Mr Berry that gave me away, his son George spoke on behalf of my brothers – they couldn't come down for the wedding, they didn't have money because it was the depression days. They were all working out on the Nullarbor, one was at the Lime Kilns and two were at the quarries, working in Naretha there.

We had my wedding breakfast home at my Mum's place ... there were only about twenty-two of us there. Afterwards my sister said we've got to have a dance and all the rest. We used to go to the dances at this parish church every Saturday when I lived down there, so they asked us did I want the church, and did I want the band on the following Saturday. Those days, any boy or girl that turned twenty-one, every girl that got married, the community gave a party. The P&C, the mother's guild, all these kind of church people they gave a party to every boy and girl that was 21 years of age. The girls all had a kitchen tea and so they gave me a kitchen tea and they asked did I want the hall for the next Saturday, and I said: "Oh yes!" I said to my husband: "What do you think?" and he said: "Oh alright."

The people who used to come to the dances all came along there as well. It was really lovely because there was modern and old-time dancing and the people, you knew them all because they were the regular ones. It was always packed out on Saturday nights. We used to have a marvellous time, and the older ladies, they would bring a plate – cakes, sandwiches and things that were all home-made. My husband, he supplied the beer there, and we got George Berry (the one who spoke on behalf of my brothers), his family worked for Watsonia … and they got the ham for sandwiches. Another chap by the name of Len Geris, got a five gallon keg of port wine and brought that over, and there was beer and cool drinks and wine … plenty of stuff.

First house

Before I went up there, the chap that was going to be my husband, my two brothers, and the chap that was best man at our wedding … Ralph Tabain, they bought a stove and built it in for me. A number one Metters stove, a black one. At least I had a stove there, not like when I was on the Kurrawang Woodline.

I didn't have a cooler then and we didn't have a double bed – we had those old Coolgardie stretchers – it was alright for the summer months, but the winter months we had to put them together, so we'd hem enough blankets to go over them. My wardrobe was made out of four bits of wood with kind of canvas around the side and wood on top and it had a wooden floor and I just put a curtain in front and we used to hang the clothes there.

All you got was mutton, not lamb, just mutton, and they carried live sheep with them on the train. In the carriage they had this kind of chute thing you could come through to where it was the butcher's shop and they'd pull the sheep out and kill the sheep there ... on the train, as they went along. More often than not instead of being firm it was all floppy, not long been killed, and we just got it like that. It used to be kind of tough. In the winter months you could order a bit of beef ... they'd carry some, but only in the winter months.

I used to get a big lump of topside all in one piece and this old lady, Mrs Lowe, told me, she said: "Get the water boiling, Jean." She lived on the line ... her husband was a ganger on the railways, and they didn't have refrigerators or anything. She said to get this big saucepan full of boiling water ... throw in a hand of salt and when that boils, dump in the meat and just leave it for a minute or two so that it seals all the outside of it. Then I used to keep that in the cooler, and that kept good for a couple of days. And then when you cut it, inside it was just like it was really fresh. But in the winter months I used to order a sirloin and steak. I could never think in the line of pounds, I said I want one about so thick. But when they got those refrigerated vans on, you got everything, pork, beef and all.

The old Tea and Sugar train

The old Tea and Sugar train would come in all hours of the night and we'd be buzzing around in the dark. I went down there once with two different shoes on, good job the heels were the same. Someone said: "Look at your shoes". I got them for the right foot, but they were different shoes. I nearly fell over when I saw that myself. How I managed to get the ones for the right feet I don't know. You just leave your pyjamas or nightie on and put a dressing gown on and the first one who hears … mostly if a man was firing he'd always keep tab. One would start at 6 o'clock and another at 6 in the night and they take over for 12-hour shifts when the kilns were burning, otherwise they only worked eight hours a day.

When we came – the Tea and Sugar train – it's not like now, I think they have it all set up like a shop – well they didn't then, they had a van, but you always sent an order. When you received one order, you sent another order in, and they brought everything that you ordered, and you took your order like that. But when we first went up there, Charlie Eaton used to be our van man then and he would stay in Naretha, because in Naretha they have the quarries working there and they had a lot of men working. There were about eighty odd men because the quarries were run by the Commonwealth Railways and they had ballast for the railway line there, and then they had a ramp made of sleepers. The van used to stay there, the Tea and Sugar train would shunt it off, and they would go further on the Rawlinna and to Cook. There you could buy some extra vegetables, and they would have some shirts and things like that that most of the men used to buy. I never saw any of them at the kilns buying clothes or anything like that, but they'd have some shirts … odds and ends of things like that but not set up like a proper shop.

We mostly ordered our vegies and then we used afterwards to get our vegies from Ehlers, down past Saunders. Ehlers used to have a kind of greengrocery shop and they used to send boxes of vegetables out along the line. We'd order what we want, and they'd pack it in the box, in those boxes like I said were made into my cupboards there, and send it out. Once a week we used to get it, but we always tried to be a fortnight's supply ahead, especially in the line of tinned stuff … plenty of potatoes, onions and flour and some tinned stuff, and we always had chooks.

Mr and Mrs Keasey that were there – she had her two brothers that were working there and another chap by the name of Mr Bostleman – he was a fireman – he came from Spearwood and was firing out there. And there was others, the three boy Donovans – and one of the boy Donovans' wife, Alice, she was there too, and there was Mrs Hales, and just myself, and a Mrs Zuvela – no relation to my husband, but the same name.

We had a bush shower and had to conserve water

We had no water there whatsoever – the firm used to send water out in the gins – 9000 gallon gins I think they were – the Commonwealth Railways would bring it out from Kalgoorlie – the scheme water. Sometimes if the dam was full at Zanthus we'd get some from Zanthus. And when we were getting short we'd tell the agent in town and they'd send it out and we'd cart it on a tank on the truck and pump it into tanks. When I first went there we had three forty-four gallon petrol drums on a stand and you put a bucket or a dish under it. You weren't short of water – there was plenty to wash yourself, do the washing and cooking, but there was none to put on a garden.

The rinsing water or bath water was put into a forty-four gallon drum and they mixed it with the lime ash stuff – it made like cement, and they put that on the floor of the kitchen or the bedroom part. It was only bag and filter cloth walls, all whitewashed. Some of them only had bags opened up and sewn up and then the iron roof. And some of them had sleeper floors. No matter how often the floors were swept there was always lime ash dust – it was better to sweep up first and dust afterwards. We sprinkled it with water to lay the dust, but it was easier than having to walk on the dirt.

So on washing day I'd leave what hot water was in the copper, sweep, then throw buckets of water over the sleeper floor and go over it with a broom – then clean water.

If a sea breeze came in it would come over the dumps and you could hear the breeze coming for a long way before it came to the camp. That's what I missed in Kalgoorlie – you missed all the nice sunsets you used to see, and you could hear that sea breeze before it got there. You could see the dust, and someone would yell: "Shut the windows".

Working with lime is dusty, and I will admit that when you perspired, a lot of you got whitey as if there was flour all over you. But when the men came home from work they mostly wiped all the surplus dust off them, and if you rubbed olive oil on your face, neck and arms where the dust was, leave it for a little while, then wash yourself in warm water, you'd never know you'd ever worked in the lime. When you washed there'd still be a whitish dust on you, but not after the olive oil. I suppose any oil would have done – but Slavs and Italians, we use or cook in olive oil. I don't buy dripping or anything like that, I generally use olive oil. Instead of putting butter on my beans, I put olive oil – not in potatoes; I put butter in that.

Life was hard, but your days were full, because the kiln was very close to where you lived. The men's smoko time, about half-past nine, was really their breakfast. They'd start work at say seven o'clock or half past, they'd have a cup of coffee. I had two nephews boarding with me and another older man, my husband and myself. They'd only have coffee and a slice of toast and go off to work and then by nine or half-past, I had their breakfast cooked there and would put it on the table as they stepped inside the door. And that was no sooner finished and you'd have to think of lunch, because they knocked off at twelve until one. My mother used to say: "I never saw such a place ... it's all meals!" We were

Glimpses of Jean

busy all the time. People I worked for years ago, one of the girls said, gee … you'd have nothing to do.

There were men that were bachelors, and the original crowd that came up there, well some of them, Mrs Keasey done cooking for them. First, they went into tents before they built a new place. That place was bag and a lime ashy kind of floor and iron on the top, because they brought a lot of stuff with them when they came up to start off.

The biggest camp would have been about four rooms, that's the biggest there, just bags and filtercloth and all the bags were sewn together.

The Keasey brothers were German. Their real name was Keaseybata … Charlie Keasey came over here from Germany when he was two years old to South Australia, and then I don't know what age he was when he came over here, but he had relations in South Australia. Him and his wife went over for a holiday and their relations must have a butcher's shop, because they got the cousin to send some nice German sausages over.

Mostly at Kurrawang, I was by myself

We went out to Kurrawang in February and came back the following February. When I got out to Kurrawang, there was just my husband and I and we stayed out in the gang he was working for, chopping engine wood for the train – they used to call it the 'rake' – and it brought the timber in for the mines. I just cooked for him and I there. I had turned twenty-six by then, and had my twenty-seventh birthday in the May and we left in the following February and went back to the Lime Kilns.

For nine months, I just lived out in the gang where the men were, and I was most of the day by myself. They were cutting wood for the train, and the others there would be cutting timber for the mines. One

Slav fellow who came from the same village as Mark did, he was driving one of the trucks, and sometimes he would come out to load up on the truck to go and pick up the wood there. Some days I might go and cook something, and then walk out to the bush where they were chopping wood, and just give Mark a hot meal there, and I'd have my dinner with him and I'd walk home.

We had two tents, one was our bedroom and the other, a ten by eight, that was our kitchen. I had one of those little tin safes, and I had it on a small table. I had to put the legs in tins of water and a little bit of kerosene, because the ants would climb up. We had a beer case with some blocks of wood and they cut them down and you could sit as if you sat at the table like a chair – that was our chairs. We had two of those. Then my husband got some gimlet wood – that gimlet's very hard – and he put in little bolts, and out of a beer case he made the top of a table and the frame of the thing was out of gimlet wood with just bolts through it. That was my table. I had boxes for my tinned stuff, but I never had a cooler.

We used to get meat twice a week. And a chap used to come out with water – he'd have those hundred or two hundred gallon square tanks and they'd put the water in the tanks for us, and with your bucket you went down and got buckets full as you needed it. You might have to walk from here to across the road. You could have as much as you liked, it wasn't rationed, and you didn't have to be as careful about the water there as when we first went to the Lime Kilns.

I had a tub and a scrubbing board and my copper was a kerosene tin on this open fire, and I got a set of those mother potts irons. You know the lids of those forty-four gallon drums, well I got one and belted it and bent some of the side up a bit – it was more oblong in the finish, the way I knocked it up. Then I found a couple of stones, it was one stone really, and my husband kind of cracked it in halves and I used to light the fire, put those two stones down there and then lay this iron thing across the top and put the mother pots iron on that to heat. Then I'd take my little table from the tent near the fire – the open fireplace was outside – and I'd do my ironing out there, because the irons were close.

It was out in the sun there and I used to make lasagne – like that macaroni, it's only flour and eggs and water – and to dry it I used to put down brown paper or tea towel after I'd made it and cut it and put it out there and just move it around a bit there until the sun dried it … on my table out in the sun.

But mostly there, I was by myself. My husband worked on the gang for about nine months. I just cooked for my husband and myself. I read what I could get and fancy-worked like mad. When payday came we'd walk into the main camp and my husband knew a couple of chaps there. I couldn't speak Slav those days, though I understood what they were talking about, and sometimes we would have our lunch with these couple of Slavs and they'd be talking away, and one had a gramophone and I used to play the records. They had mostly Slav records but I can understand them, so I had the music there.

I went in another time to the main camp with my husband and one Slav fellow came up to me, because I said where my mother comes from – it's Zlarin – and they call the women Zlarinka, and this Slav fellow said: "Are you a Zlarinka?" I said: "Yes", although I'm Australian, but I'm descended from there, and he said: "There's a chap down there that knows you". I went down and it was a fellow that my stepfather helped to bring out from the old country. He was working on the garden for a while at Spearwood with us until he got a job and then he was up at the woodline. The last I heard of him he was working on the mines at Norseman, and he got sick and he died down there.

There weren't any other women at the camp, but that didn't worry me – I got on well with the men. They were mostly all Slavs – there was only one Italian fellow there and the rest were Slavs. One must have been many years in Australia, old Mr Starcevich, and you know he used to have a little wireless, like a crystal thing, and it was made out of a Pasha coffee tin – it had a Turkish bloke on it called Pasha. And that little tin was a wireless. You'd have to put it in your ear and you'd hear music or something and yet there was no aerial or anything … I don't know how it happened, but through crystals or something he made it work. He spoke very good English; he must have been out here for years and years.

We used to play bluff poker a lot … until two or three o'clock in the morning. We had a kerosene tin and they'd put chips in and we'd get nice hot coals, and put it under the table that was made out of gimlet, and when it got a bit down we'd put in another chip or something just to keep our feet warm. That's the only way we could keep warm. It was cold, but when you got into bed it was alright.

When we lived up at the Lime Kilns, the Tea and Sugar would be blowing the whistle quite a bit as they came to the siding, because it'd come in at two or three in the morning, sometimes. It was funny, it must have been three or four months I was living out there at Kurrawang in this gang, and I heard the whistle of the train and I gave my husband a dig and said: "Quick Mark, light the light, there's the train". And I sat up and said: "It's alright, you can go back to sleep, I thought I was at the Lime Kilns". I still had it in my head that when I heard that whistle I had to get up and go down to the siding to get my meat and goods!

The rest as I say were Slavs. They'd come over some evenings and we'd sit outside and talk of this and that, and those who could speak English I'd speak English to. The boss was an Aussie bloke; Jack Grace his name was. I think he was a Commo because when he got drunk he used to say: "The flag is as red as deep as red" – I can't remember the rest of it. He came over one day. "Mark," he said, "Come over here and look." He had Khaki clothes on and he had put his sheets in a kerosene tin, and the khaki things, and he'd put all his sheets and things all out on bushes (he didn't have a clothes line) … he said: "Look, everything, bloody khaki". He'd boiled them together, and the sheets where they should have been white were all khaki. He used to get a little bit shot, but he was always a gentleman. I found none of them were any trouble.

Then we got shifted into the main camp

There were lots of women at the main camp, and we were three months there. They had a store and it was on a train thing – a proper store, you could go and get your groceries. You just went up and asked Julius, an Italian, and get your meat and stuff there. Not long before I shifted into the main camp, I'd planted some lettuce because I'd thought we'd be longer in the other camp, and I said to my husband: "I'm going to walk out to the old camp to see if the lettuce has come up", and I went and it was about five inches high. I broke some of the lettuces off and brought them back and showed him. There was a track where the truck used to go so I wouldn't lose myself.

Up the end where I was, there was only one other lady and I on that side, we were mostly up one end and as you come in on the train, our camps were the first. On the other side of the railway line, there was another couple of Slavs, but when you went down there was a very big camp, and in the main camp there were other Slav and Italian women.

I got papers there from anybody after I went into the main camp. Mum lived in Kalgoorlie and she'd send out stuff for me to read. She lived for a while in Piccadilly Street; they had a couple of bedrooms and a kitchen part, just opposite the power station. When Mark and I came in for one Christmas, the lady had one spare room and she said we could have that for the week while we were in town. We still had the steam trains then, and we used to get on that. Afterwards, Mum rented a house up in Addis street, from Mrs Allen I think her name was, and I think Mr Tomich used to live on the corner in a brick place facing Graeme and Addis Street. A Mrs Hunt used to live next door – Hunts used to have Watsonia's butter. We used to get butter and eggs from Hunts up in Hannan street. We got ham too. After we got it from Stiles, Stahls or something like that. We used to get a whole side of bacon once a month, and you could boil that with cabbage and potatoes etc.

I was at the main camp one day and it was thunder and lightning and I'm frightened of it … I saw a big jarrah tree blown up one day when I was eight years old and it scared the devil out of me. There was a lady there, she was one of 'them girls', and some of the men that were friends of my husband and came from his village said: "You don't want to be seen talking with her". But she used to come down to my place because at that end of the camp was only us two and she used to bring some books down, those love tales. Anyway this day of thunder and lightning, I was scared so I went up there and even though they said: "You don't want to go up there, you'll get a bad name for yourself", I said I didn't care, so long as I had somebody to be with. I was only living in a tent. I'm still frightened, when I'm in the house and there's thunder and lightning, I'm like that. I'm just scared of it. I saw that tree and it stuck in my head. I've been the same ever since. Even when I was out in the Lime Kilns and my husband was night firing he'd go out and put a fire out and walk home just to stay with me because he knew I was scared of it. It's stupid I suppose.

Anyway, I went up to sit with this woman, and she said: "You never come to my place" and I didn't know what to say because of what my husband told me. She said, if people knew what it was like for girls to work in brothels they'd never go there. But she said, "I was forced to go, I had kids to look after." She was living with an Italian fellow, but she was a prostitute in the past. She said she had kiddies. Apparently she had been married and her husband must have left her and she had the kids to look after so she said, "I had to". But that's what she said, if they knew what it was like, none of the girls would go into that type of life. If she spoke, I spoke to her, and her life was nothing to do with me. If she wants to live it that way it's her business.

A lot of sly grogging used to go on

You met all types, there was Italians and Slavs there, and a lot of sly grogging used to go on in those days. One Slav family – I knew them but I never went to their place – but they tell me they used to have chooks and they had a beer box dug in the ground and they used to leave the beer up there. She used to go and put the bucket in as if she was taking the stuff up to the chooks, and bring the bottle of beer down to the house. They all did it. It was an extra few bob there and I suppose for the men that were bachelors, it was somewhere for them to go. They'd play cards, and get a bottle of beer or a bottle of wine.

A friend of my husband's there, he got caught. He was sitting there, and he couldn't get rid of it; they came in and he had half a glass of beer in front of him so he had to go to court. That was a long time ago. He wasn't drunk or anything, but a lot of them did it. It was just a kind of respectable thing for some of them.

When we were out at Kurrawang wood line Mr Geere wanted another kiln built at the Lime Kilns out at Naretha, and my husband asked for leave – a week or two to put the foundation down – but the boss at Kurrawang, Tom Valli, wouldn't let him go. So the agent said to

Mark would he at least come and lay the foundation and tell them what to do. Then we wrote and told old Mr Geere who then got on to the Lake View and Star Mine who wrote out to Tom Valli, and he came looking for my husband one day and he said: "If you want to go you can – why didn't you tell me it was for the Lake View and Star?" My husband said: "Well you didn't give me a chance". He said: "If you want, you can go altogether". But my husband said they only wanted him for a week, and was told he could go and stay as long as he liked – until he had finished. He stayed and finished the whole kiln and then he came back. I stayed with my mother there in Kalgoorlie while he went back to the Lime Kilns.

When he came back to the Kurrawang Woodline, in about 1936, there was a big strike on out there, and it didn't seem as if they were going to finish, so we went back to the Lime Kilns. We had waited there for about two or three weeks, and then my husband went down and said that he was going to leave. He said, "It's no good me just staying here and doing nothing." The manager said "You can go to work", and my husband said: "No, staying here and doing nothing I'm no friend of yours, and if I go to work I'm not friends with my friends". So he said "I'm going".

Chapter 3
Life on the Kilns

Exterior of a Lime Kilns home

The Keasey Brothers were German...

When we came back from Kurrawang we went into another tent, because somebody else had that other camp we had lived in. We went into the place that used to be a boarding house, because Mr Keasey had left. There were two Keasey brothers, George and Charlie. Charlie was the one that mostly stayed at the Kilns. George was up there in the early stages when they first started the Lime Kilns, and one of his daughters came up and done cooking for some of the men that were batching. They were mostly Aussies, with this other Yugoslav chap, Mr Andy Zuvela. The original crowd that came up there, well she done cooking for them. The place was only bag and a lime ashy kind of floor and iron on the top, because they brought a lot of stuff with them when they came up to start off.

Some people went away and I bought a kitchenette and a table and the chairs. That kitchen setting belonged to Mrs Hales, she left. That kitchenette and table and chairs, four chairs, it cost seven pounds ten new – I forget what I paid. The table I had out at Kurrawang, I took that out there too.

Then I bought a table from a lady in Naretha – a big table, a beautiful white one – wood about that thick, and with those carved legs on. You could put four people on each side, at a push, and one each at the end. When I first bought it, it had all rings there where they'd had the paint tin. Well, you don't know how much trouble I had to get those rings of paint off. I used to scrub it every day with that old sandsoap, and then I'd buy lemons from the train and I'd put salt and lemon juice and rub it all over. Old Mr Geeres saw that table like it was before, and after I'd scraped the paint off and he said: "Look Jean, you wouldn't believe that was the same table". When I left, I gave the table and another big kitchenette to another lady on a station on the Trans Line.

Everybody would get dressed up

Years ago when I was first out there, when the quarries were going, they used to have a dance in the boarding house at Naretha. They used to have a dance once a week and everybody would get dressed up, and properly, because in those days it was long frocks fad. They'd get dressed up in proper evening clothes, and the men too, and they'd have a dance. The women would bring a plate and we'd go in the old Model-T Ford.

The boss, he had a Studebaker car for him and his wife, and those who got in first, would get a ride in the Studebaker car. I had a couple of rides in it, and the other men would go in the old Model-T Ford. They had a pianola, and a chap by the name of Jack Stanford, he used to play the piano. One Slav chap, who used to work at the Lime Kilns, he used to play the piano accordion, and we had modern and old-time dancing. It was really nice.

With my brothers there I didn't mind doing the washing because I used to think the sun shone out of my brothers. I had two of those tubs and a washing board that you rubbed like nobody's business. I had a tinny one at first but then I got a glass one after. I used to ask the boss's wife out there could I have a lend of her copper and I used to go down there, and there was a great big mulga tree, and she had her copper there. Her husband made a kind of bench. I carted my own water all from my drums. I wouldn't go to your place and take the water from you. I carted it from about here to across the road, in buckets. We had kerosene tins. I never carried it on a yoke, like the Chinese used to. That's a good idea carrying it that way, and you wouldn't have all that weight ... you just support it, that's all.

Nobody knows but when my brothers left the Lime Kilns up there – it really hurt, because we were so close. When we got married the older brother left and he went to work for the Commonwealth Railways at the quarries at Naretha. Frank, the second oldest brother, he left the Lime Kilns and went into Naretha too because he said it's no good to live with a married couple, because he said blood's thicker than water – there could be arguments and I know who I'd stick up for so he said that way you fight your own battles.

Every chance I had to go into Naretha because in those days the trains came at about half-past nine at night and I used to go in when anybody went in with the mail. Often a lady that turned out to be my eldest brothers Auntie by marriage afterwards, old Mrs Lowe, she used to say: "Jean's in – I can hear them talking down there at the camp", because my brothers' camps weren't far away. The driver used to drop me off at my brother's camps and I'd yap away like mad.

Old Jim Geere was our first agent – Jack Johnston (the bike people), Carmel (Jack's wife), she used to be old Mr Geere's secretary. And then Hodgston and Cranston took over the agency for the lime from him, because old Mr Geere retired. Some of the managers – Cam Shaw was one – something to do with the mines out there – and there were some others too in it – they formed a company and they bought the Lime Kilns and then old Mr Geere got out of it – or died – and what shares Mr Geere had, they allowed my husband to buy, and so we had a small share.

Later on another man came along to manage it, but he didn't know much about lime, so Mr Hales managed it for a while, but then they left. After one more manager, my husband got the job – in the war years. One young chap who managed for a couple of weeks was a bush mechanic – you may remember Albert Paolocchi – he had Supreme Motors in Kalgoorlie.

Glimpses of Jean

Brown paper and string

All I ever used to do was fancy work – that's living in the bush – just fancy work and reading – I think if I didn't have my fancy work and reading I'd have gone up the wall. I said if I could read brown paper I would have read that too. My husband used to say that if only I was with money like I was with brown paper and string … you couldn't go to the shop where we lived, there was no shop. You ordered your stuff off the Tea and Sugar train and you always kept a fortnight ahead of yourself in the food line. And you couldn't run across to the shop there – you'd borrow from one another.

Even in the line of money – we didn't work for the Commonwealth Railways and we had to pay cash and always somebody had a couple of hundred pounds in the camp and you'd say "I'll go to so and so, he or she will have it". Then next payday would come along and you'd just give it back – you never locked your place up, but now you've got to lock everything there. But I used to save brown paper and string – even rope. I'd undo the knots and think I might need that. Out in the bush sometimes, you couldn't go and get a ball of string. I used to flatten the brown paper out and put it away, and it was all kept because if I needed a parcel I had brown paper to wrap it in – or I'd put it in the bottom of tins if I was making a fruit cake or something like that.

A couple of times I had to go to Perth. I got an abscess in my face once and another time I got bad kidney trouble and I stayed with old Mrs Reed (Ron's mother) – they had that shop just cross from the Town Hall in Boulder. I stayed with her for 2 or 3 weeks – I didn't know any doctors or anybody, although I'd lived in Boulder and started school there when I was six.

That is the only Lime Kilns out there. They said they were going to put another one at Parkeston, but it cost too much and apparently it'd only work two or three days and then be idle too much, and then they let it go.

One young chap who managed for a couple of weeks was a bush mechanic – his name was Arthur Lowe. Well, some of the trucks there had got crook, and this Arthur Lowe fixed them. He was very good at fixing trucks and when my husband came to Kalgoorlie once he met another fellow there and he said: "You must have a good mechanic there", and my husband said: "He only talks to the trucks and those trucks will go".

Arthur was telling us that when he was a kid, at Tarcoola, his father was a ganger on the railways. The schoolteacher wanted to take him to Adelaide to get him apprenticed to a mechanic, but his mother wouldn't let him go. He wouldn't sleep at night until he had fathomed a problem out. He could take and engine out and put it back a lot quicker than some of these nowadays and he never went to school or anything. He just loved it – would read up everything about it. We had about four trucks out there and another chap had a utility, and we had a utility of our own. When we first went out there they had model-T Fords. Then they bought a 4x4 from the army, then they had a diesel truck. The Slav blokes used to call our utility 'The Warrior'.

It was in the war years that we got the pedal radio – after we had a big storm there. We had about 5 or 6 inches of rain within not much over an hour and there was water everywhere. There was damage to the kilns – one was full of cooked lime ready to be bagged and the water just poured into that and all the lime went all slack and everything. The other kiln had only been lit up that morning and the day was lovely and sunny in the morning, but by the afternoon it just thundered and lightning and the rain just poured down – water everywhere, and that kiln, it was put out where the water came over the draught.

In the war years there was always trains going. I know I met my brother on one of them. I wasn't supposed to know, but I got to know he was on the train and went in to see him. He was coming back to get married and my mother just said: "Tom'll be coming through". We had a couple of letters that I sent down that got censored. I suppose they just took random ones from here and there.

A Spitfire crashed

Another thing that happened out there in 1944 ... a Spitfire crashed about 12 miles north from our camp. One day I said to Mum, who was staying there, "These planes, four or five of them came flying just over our camp and made a bee-line straight to the railway line and turned around and zoomed straight out west and low flying. I wonder what they're doing there?"

She said, "I suppose they're coming from somewhere".

I said: "But there's nowhere up that way ... the planes generally come from the east, but its odd to come straight from north and down like that and quickly turn there". And then later in the evening, a chap from Rawlinna came down and a couple from Naretha to say that a plane had come down and would we go to help with the search, because we had the trucks and gas producers then. It was not the ones Mum and I saw, but one that was with them, and the other planes went straight on to town. I think they flew right from where the other bloke had crashed.

And they said would my husband go out with the truck and see if they could find them. They said it was just a few miles north from us and another plane came out to be a spotter. They had the green and orange and red lights and said they'd put such and such a light down when they arrived to show us where they were.

Of course, silly me, we went out and the sea breeze came in that night and we nearly died with the cold, it was that bitterly cold. We put a mattress on the back of the truck as well. We were going through bush we hadn't gone through before and with only a gas producer. And anyway it got really late and was getting dark and my brother-in-law wouldn't drive the truck any more. My husband and another chap by the name of Alec Absalom and another fellow – I can't think of the other fellow's name – they started to walk as much as they could to follow that plane. And the pilot of the spotter plane had said, if he finds the missing plane, he would drop a flare down as he only had enough juice to get him back to Kalgoorlie.

It was still daylight but it was getting darkish, and the spotter plane did find the plane so my husband and the other two blokes, they just stayed there the night, where they were. The plane dropped the flare just before dark. They couldn't go on because they had no lights. In the morning my husband took notice of a big tree … he said: "It was over that way", and the others said: "Go this way", so my husband went his way and the others went theirs, but the three of them kept close to one another.

I wasn't with them – I stayed where the truck was, but my brother-in-law and a couple of other men, they walked on.

Anyway, my husband spotted it there, and they found a young fellow. He was all right, but the plane was upside down. My husband said the hole he got out of, you wouldn't have thought a cat could get out of it. The pilot said he tried to land on this flat – there's lots of flats out there just like as if it's an aerodrome. But he said there was one stump in that flat and the plane hit it and he turned right over … the engine kind of shot out of the plane from the force of it. Apparently that was the second time he'd crashed. He'd crashed once up at Darwin.

Anyway, my husband and the two others and the pilot, they started walking and they walked and walked and walked and Mark thought they were going the wrong way. But the majority said no, and of course the poor pilot was going with them, and they came to some country and he saw gum trees and said, "We're going the wrong way". Of course, where we are it's only that mulga country there. They said, "How do you know?" and he said: "We're where the gum trees are, and that's out of the way. We should be where there's only all mulga". And he said, "I'm not going any further" and that he'd go south. And he went straight south and they got to the railway line and in that time there was a section car coming up and down between the 926-mile and Naretha, patrolling, in case anyone turned up.

A bit later a plane did come out and circled where the plane was still crashed, but there was nobody there. I thought: "Oh God they're all lost!" and it was summer, I was nearly crying. We didn't know which way to go, so in the morning we'd come home – my brother-in-law was driving. Anyway the section car bloke came along and brought the three men home and the pilot as well, and the plane came out from the air force base there and picked up the pilot. They wouldn't let us give him any dinner or anything, they just said he could have some weak tea with sugar, and that's all he had. He was quite OK – I think he broke a finger or something.

Those other three men, I can still see Mum cooking them bacon and eggs to give them a feed, but they wouldn't let the pilot have anything. They just said he could have a cup of tea. He went into our bedroom and the Doctor examined to see that he was all right and he said not to give him anything, just a cup of tea. Then they flew him into town.

Two or three days later the air force crowd came up with a big semi trailer and a truck with one of those square tanks for water on it. My husband went with them to take them out to where the plane crashed and they stripped it all down and put it all on the semi-trailer and took it to Kalgoorlie to the air force base. When we came in to Kalgoorlie there they told us that the plane was one of their actual Spitfires that had fought in the Battle of Britain. One of the officers that came out said to call and see them at the base, so we called in and had a cup of tea and showed us around the base. Phil Scattini took us around, he was out there then; he died not long ago Phil did.

That happened I think in September of 1944, and none of that was put in the paper or anything. It was real excitement. It was good that we found the bloke all right and it was a happy ending – it could have been worse, he could have been killed – it was just lucky. I don't remember his name, and it wasn't in the papers. That was all war business, and it was only that we were there, or maybe we wouldn't have known anything. It was just lucky we were the only ones that had trucks and could go out.

Meat and butter…and keeping it cool

We had a waterbag … an old waterbag that's hung up and we'd cut a bit off and leave a part just like a pocket thing here and I used to put the butter in a jar and a little bit of water in the waterbag and have a wet cloth around it and have a lid on top of the jar and sit my butter in the thing. It would be an old waterbag – you'd keep it damp with a wet cloth and it'd hang up there. The way my kitchen was made was just like a breezeway. When the sea breeze was in we used to have a blind made out of bags with a lump of wood through the bottom and we could roll it up in the daytime, and let it down when the strong breeze came through. I used to hang the water bag up in there, and when it dried I wet the cloths again and put it round the butter.

If the Tea and Sugar came on Tuesdays, I'd just buy enough that we'd have fresh meat that night for tea. I'd generally get a leg because there was more meat on that and I'd partly roast that and that'd be all right. Then the next night I'd cook the meat right through and have a roast dinner, and then what meat was left over, I'd make a potato pie out of it.

I used to cook the meat and I had, you know, those tin dishes that come up in a bowl kind of fashion, and I'd put a cloth just over the top of that and put a cloth inside and put the meat in that. That's all I had, and I'd put it up high. But at that time we had a lot of wild cats out there and they got to the meat one night there, and the meat had gone. I'd put it on a box on the table and the dish on top of that … stupid me, coming from the town, I didn't know the cats were as bad as that.

I don't know where I got it from, but later somebody gave me a little safe, a little tin one, and we hung the leftover meat in that breezeway. I even brought that little safe to Kalgoorlie with me when we left. But we got this little safe, and the next morning another woman who was living in the camp was close to where I was living at first – she and I could smell this smell and I looked everywhere and I couldn't make out where it came from. I never thought about the meat. And I said to this girl: "God, Flo, you wouldn't think it would be the meat would it?" I should have gone there first; it was bluey green. It was finished.

When they had floods after that big storm, we didn't have meat at all for a couple of weeks there. They dropped a sheep from a section car for the Commonwealth Railways people, but we never got anything at all. We weren't working on the railways, and so they got it. They thought we'd got some and we said, no, we never got anything at all. And then the train did come down from Rawlinna, the engine did, and we sent a message to them to bring some stuff down. Got the ganger to ring up for us. We went into Naretha and collected some groceries in the line of tinned stuff, so we could have plenty of that on hand.

If you've got tinned sausages or bully beef – I used to fry up some onions and tinned tomatoes, and put the bully beef in and cook a pot of macaroni. Well you can throw them all together and grate some cheese on top. It was a meal, not that I liked it, but as long as you've got potatoes, onions and tinned stuff, you can make do. Jiggle it around somehow and make a meal.

Chapter 4
People of the Kilns

Jean

Scotty's false teeth

There was fellow, we called him Scotty, he came from Kalgoorlie to work out there and he liked his booze. Once he'd come into town and was coming home one night on the train, on the fast goods, and he must have been sick and he lost his false teeth down the toilets. He told the guard where he thought he lost those teeth, and said for the ganger to keep his eyes open. And he told us that about a week alter, the guard on the train handed him one of those Commonwealth Railway envelopes, and inside was Scotty's false teeth.

Another time there was and Englishman, a Pommie chap – his name was Bob, and him and Scotty, and an Aussie called Frank, and they got on the booze. A few days went by and they told my husband that Bob up there had cut his foot and he had maggots in his foot. Anyway my husband could hardly believe it. He went up and he really did have maggots there, and Mark said: "You had better go to town". He washed it all out with solyptol and bandaged it up. We didn't have a medical chest or no pedal radio in those days. In their drunkenness – they had a ten-gallon keg – he must have broken a bottle or a glass. And my husband got the keg and threw it out the door, and he said "You'll have to go to town". Well, no way, he wasn't going to town. He said: "You can fix me up Mark". Well every day Mark used to go up there and bathe that foot, but he always limped afterwards.

This other Aussie bloke, Frank, had false teeth, and he lost his teeth and for days and days he'd go around and kick over every little mound of dirt looking for his false teeth, and he never found them from that day to this. He got another set after. But then he left the Lime Kilns.

Then once after, we had a Yugoslav fellow there, I can't think of his name, but he got lost. He was a woodcutter and he just went bush and one of the drivers came and said: "Is so and so home?" And we said no, and they went to his camp and he wasn't home and they went out looking. The schoolmaster, he came out from Naretha and wanted to go, Stan Jones I think his name was, and he wrote home to his mother and he said: "I'm just going on a man hunt". And so, they started off, and they went out to dark, as far as they could, about sixteen miles away from the camp in the direction where this man was cutting wood and couldn't find him.

So, we had to get on to the police and they sent out a policeman and a black tracker. At that time they had some blacks at the camps – periodically they used to come along like – and anyway they loaded up one of the trucks. So anyway the police came out and this tracker, they started out, and they thought he went west, going bush. The tracker and another aboriginal, they just ran behind the truck, and my husband said he couldn't see anything, but then they'd say: "Look that's where he sat; that's where the heel of his foot was". They went along and the tracker stopped and called the police over, and the man had taken off his underpants and buried it near a rabbit hole in soft dirt, but he wouldn't touch it until the police came along. Then they went on; they still hadn't found him and they must have done about sixty miles, and then they crossed over the railway line … the bloke was going west, and crossed over the railway line, and they found him and picked him up and brought him back to the camp. He had his clothes on, but the other things he had, his water bag and his axe, they never found them from that day to this. Nobody knows why he buried his underpants – he never spoke or nothing, but he did speak to me when they got in the truck. He just said goodbye in the truck and that's all he said – he couldn't speak much English. The policeman went over while he shaved himself and stayed with him for a while.

They were back in time to catch the train, because in those days we could stop the passenger train at the siding. You had a disc that you held up and the train would stop. Afterwards they cut that out and we'd have to go to Naretha – we were ten miles from Naretha. Anyway, they were in time to take this chap to town and they had him in hospital for a while and then he got all right ... apparently there were mental disturbances in that family. When he got better, he went out to the Kurrawang Woodline – whether it was Kurrawang or Lakewood I'm not sure, but he got lost again. Then they sent him away afterwards to Heathcote, and he was there for a while and then he turned up at a cousin's place in Fremantle. In the finish they sent him back to the old country. A cousin of his went the same way, and they sent him back to Yugoslavia.

Women at the kilns

In the long run there were Slav women at the Lime Kilns and one Dutch woman and her husband. There has been Slavs, English, Irish, Italian and Dutch people have worked out there. My sister in-law doesn't speak very good English even today and she'd been out here for quite a while because her daughter is thirty-four, and she was born out here. The other ones couldn't speak English – they have gone down around Middle Swan way and Spearwood now. The Dutch girl could speak English very well, and she and her husband left and worked on the Commonwealth Railways, and they got a job out where we were. Then they went over to South Australia.

Most of the time I had other women out there, though in those days I couldn't speak Slav, I could only understand it, and when those two English women left and there was only Slavs, I mostly done my reading. I'd listen to them for a while and then I'd go home to bed. I knew what they were talking about, but I couldn't talk back. They'd talk about things in the Old Country. Years later, when I went to Yugoslavia and came back, well then I could speak about their village because I knew a lot of people who they used to talk about, and by then I could speak Slav. I'd learnt after the war years how to speak Yugoslav, so I didn't feel out of it.

The only really good friend I had out there was one Australian girl, but the she left. She married a Yugoslav chap and she married an Australian boy after. She was in Naretha – her sister had the boarding house and she worked there and then she came out to the Lime Kilns and then went down Nollamara way.

I saw them come and go and I'd still be there. Some of them would be there two or three years or more, especially the Slav women. My sister-in-law, well she had two kiddies born, and they started school at Rawlinna, so she was out there for a few years before she ever came into town. She came out from the old country there and she was in the family way and both the children were born in Kalgoorlie. The sister-in-law, she got bitten by a scorpion once, and that made her sick, so they caught the train into town and the doctor gave her an injection. She was OK after that.

She was married to my husband's brother – he brought him out from Yugoslavia just the year before the war started. He came in March 1938 and then he brought his wife out a year or so after the war, but they had a lot of trouble to bring her out. They authorities said first she could come, and then they said she couldn't. Then they said she could come on her own without the son, and then the son could go without her. Anyway, in the end she had to come on her own, and my husband said: "Well we'd better let her come out". He said the son, being a boy, might be able to get out like a lot of the others who'd run away and got on boats and went across to Italy. He was fifteen when he came out. He came out legally in the end – he didn't have to run away. The brother-in-law had paid the fare, but his permit expired, and we had to reapply for that again. He came out with another chap who used to be here before and had gone back home with another Yugoslav fellow. He'd found he didn't like it there because it had gone Communist, and so he came back, and the nephew came with him.

When my husband bought his nephew out here – the nephew told his wife … she had a little girl and she was in the family way with another one, he said: "It'll be four to five years at the most. Either you'll be here or I'll be home". And he kept to his word and brought her out here. And they're alright now, their children are married and they live at South Coogee, out from Spearwood – they've settled alright.

My husband helped a distant cousin to come out as well, and they had four children, but they didn't stay long because three of the kiddies went to Coolgardie convent. The boy was a little bit older, and seeing they were out in the bush, the sisters took them for a while, but then the wife didn't like it out there and they left and they settled around Bentley and now the kids are all married.

We thought it was a dingo

There was one old Slav feller, well one day early hours of the morning we heard this funny noise – we thought it was a dingo. The dogs were barking something awful, and I said to Mark: "You'd better go and have a look – go to the kiln first and get the night fireman to go with you". I was scared and when he got down there, he found this old Slav feller, only in his pyjama pants, and he'd wet himself and he was scratching in the dirt. My husband said in Slav "Oh brother" – that's just the way they speak, they're no relation – "What are you doing down there?"

The Slav feller, Peter, said: "Where's Joe? The police are going to take me wine away" and my husband sent this other feller up to get his brother, and Mark stayed with him. So between the three of them, one carrying the hurricane lamp and the others helping him, they took him home to his camp. They said: "Now you go back to bed and stay there". My husband said to the fireman: "Now when you put a fire in the kiln, you go up and see if he's alright", because he was putting a fire in every half hour.

When the fireman got back up there, Peter had got out of bed again and was dressed. He said: "I've got to go to work". Anyway, in that time, the fireman had to go down and put another fire in, and by then it was time for him to knock off and the brother-in-law took over for the day firing. So he went straight up to Peter's camp, and Peter was sitting there on the keg beside the pump, leaning on the wall, and his hands were hanging down there. The fireman said: "Peter, what in the name of heaven are you doing there?" And he just fell on the floor and he was dead.

I don't think we had a pedal radio then, we might have, but I wouldn't swear to it. Anyway they got the police to come out, Sergeant Matthews I think. He brought the coffin as well and he stayed the night, and said we'd go up in the morning. Before that, they had picked up old Peter and they put him on his bed and wrapped the sheet around him, and put the cat outside and closed the camp. That night the police came out, and in the morning Mark and the policeman went up, and he said there were no suspicious circumstances. Peter was out in kind of bruises, as if he hit something, and the policeman said: "I've seen plenty of that – he's died of alcoholic poisoning".

He used to drink an awful lot. Of a morning he would get a basin of wine with a little bit of water, and dip bread in it ... and he'd go off to work and do a darn good day's work. He never smoked. My husband used to think if he smoked and drank like Peter did, he would have died long ago. But he died there with nothing. He must have been close to sixty. He had nothing good, only what groceries were left there, and three or four shillings on the table, and that's all he had. They took the coffin on the train, and he was buried in a pauper's grave.

A permit for the fridge

A friend of mine who was a great Laborite applied for a fridge permit and she had a little baby, only just a few weeks old, beside the little girl, and they wrote and said, no she couldn't have it. Well she was mad! She was a pretty well educated girl there, because when she had her daughter on correspondence lessons, I think Mrs Merritt was her teacher there, she said: "Oh your mother should have been a school teacher", because she was very good. I know when they came into town to live and the little girl, she was twelve then, and she went to school and she was best in her class – she was more advanced than the other kiddies. Anyway the mother wrote a letter over to the Prime Minister in Canberra, and she ended it up with: "I'd like you to come over here and see if you could put up with what we have to, meat we only get twice a week". It was a Labor government and she was a strict Laborite. She said: "How would your wives like to give your children withered vegetables?" – there were four in her family. And she said: "If that's your Labor government, you can stick to it". Two weeks after, she had a permit, but I had to wait fifteen months and there were five of us. But I had the cooler and I had it until I left. I still used the cooler even when I had the fridge.

Chapter 5
The Kilns at Work

The Kilns at work in the early 1960s

How the Lime Kilns worked

At the bottom of the kiln there are three archways and a doorway and they go in there first. Inside, they've got great big rocks called sprawlers. Above the archways they build rocks that come up as if it's a wall.

From the doorway at the bottom, you put the wood in to the back wall of the kiln, and then the sprawlers – they'd lay them across the top so that you made a little tunnel affair. You'd stack as much as you can from that door, and then you fill it from the top. Then they'd put wood in, and then according to the size of the wood – the big wood and the bigger rocks were down the bottom, and you broke the stone as you got right to the very top – the stone and the wood got smaller and smaller until the stones were only quite small on the top.

And then on the back of the kiln, they put 14 gauge kind of iron around – sheets of iron propped up with great big lumps of steel, like springs of trucks to support it there. They would chock up the doorway with sheets of iron and bag and dirt to stop any air getting in that way.

The kilns were facing to the south, so if you got a south, south-east or south-west wind it was very good for the kilns because it would draw the heat and it wouldn't take so much wood to burn – it made a good draught. If the wind was in the right position and the kiln was full, no matter if they'd finished in the middle of the day – they'd light it up because a good wind was blowing, and that saved wood as well. Whereas if you had a wind blowing from the north, the smoke used to come over the top and down on the men to work and it burnt more wood to try to heat the flames.

Firing all depends on the wind … if it's a good wind they fired less than every half an hour. You've got three what you call 'callums' to put it in and you fill them up as quick as you can, because you had to throw one bigger piece towards the end of the back of the kiln. You'd push if you could to get it right down – they've got a knack of doing it there – and you'd poke it down with this big poker and then put some more in. You'd stack the whole draught upwards as much as you could with wood, and you'd hear it roaring there. Sometimes if the wind changed they got big sheets of iron … well you'd have to change those sheets of iron.

The flame used to come through the top and you'd know then that it settled. Once that good ore kind of burnt, you could only see the glowing coals on the top and you could smell the sulphur, from the stone I suppose.

If they had a period of north winds, they'd light it, because you've got your orders for lime. You'd light it, but it was not very good, and then you'd hope for the wind to change. Sometimes it used to change, but it was not very comfortable. I know when my husband first went there he used to be a night fireman, and my second eldest brother was the day fireman so they know what it was like, working in the smoke, because it had to be done. You've got the orders and had to get the lime out. One man would start at 6 o'clock and another at 6 in the night and they take over for 12 hour shifts when the kilns were burning. Otherwise they only worked eight hours a day.

That doorway at the side – you go in there and back up these little tunnel things that you make where the wood's going to be thrown into. Underneath there you've got a draught where you pull all the first ashes out.

When the kiln's finished – when it's cooked as they say – they open the door at the bottom and take all the dirt and sand and iron away from it there and then clean all the coals out that was left. The wind soon cools it down and they start bagging from down that end – three men: one shovels, one holds the bag and the other one ties the bag up. They take it turn about – it's dusty work, and they look like convicts without the chains.

Some of the men got burnt, and you've really just got to put olive oil where it is to protect their eyes. They were supposed to wear glasses – goggles – but the men found that you perspired there and they'd rather go without the glasses. Some of them found that where their trousers came to at their ankles got a bit red and sore too. But we found that we just put olive oil to neutralise it. Some of them washed in vinegar but still had a look as if their arms had been powdered.

In the war years they not only supplied Kalgoorlie mines. Those days they had the steam engines, and the Commonwealth Railways used to buy lime as well to treat the water, and we used to send lime to Rawlinna. They had a treatment plant there to clean the water so they could use it for the engines. Rawlinna used to send lime to Loongana and to Quorn Reid on the Trans Line. But afterwards they got the diesel and they didn't need that any more.

I know in the war years once they commandeered a truck of lime and less lime came into town, and in Kalgoorlie they wondered where the truck had gone to, because the consignment note was made out for so much lime to come and it didn't come. The Commonwealth Railways said that they needed the lime, it was war years and they just took it. They paid for it afterwards, but they took it because it was really needed. They wanted it in Kalgoorlie for the gold, but sometimes there were five trains a day going across there … in the war years there was always trains going.

Chapter 6
Language and Names

The Lime Kilns in the 1960s

Luba or Ljuba?

When my father got killed in the Sons of Gwalia mine, his name was Ljuba, but on the grave – Mum's Auntie was an Aussie lady, and she couldn't spell the name properly and they thought it was Luba and they've got that on the tombstone – the 'J' left out. For English people I suppose it was easier to say Luba.

When I went for a birth certificate when I was going overseas in 1965, they said there's no such person. I said, there is, because I hadn't seen my father's grave at that time, and I said, on the off chance: "well see if there's something in the name of Luba", and they found it right way. Then I found that Mum's Auntie didn't even have my proper name spelt right – it's not Jean, it's a Slav name, 'Jerka'. She put 'Erka'.

The name, 'Zuvela' is very confusing to Australians too. Out on the Kilns, there was a Mrs Zuvela who was no relation to my husband, but had the same name. All the Zuvelas have got hyphenated names so that you know which family they come from. Our name is Zuvela-Doda – that's just your clan – you come from that.

On the Island where my husband comes from, the island of Korkula, and the village of Velaleuca, well not far from there, like Kalgoorlie and Boulder is – is a place called Blato and there are Zuvelas there. My husband's Auntie – his father's sister – she was a Zuvela-Doda, but then she married a Zuvela and his hyphenated name is Zuvela-Hourt, so she belongs to that family.

I had a phone call once from someone in Melbourne and they said something about the name Zuvela – and apparently I'm the only one up here with that name – and he said: "I'm ringing on behalf of somebody else". I said "I did hear there was a Zuvela here – my husband mentioned there – and he apparently comes from the same island my husband did. I said, "But that's all I know". And then I got another phone call and I said, "Someone rang me before from Melbourne" and he said: "That chap from Melbourne rang on my behalf". This man lives in Sydney, and he said his father was a Zuvela and his mother was a Bodanovich – Bodakovich (I can't remember which) and she came from Boulder and was born in 1910, and he said: "I don't know if she's alive or dead." Apparently they had never married, and he only found out not long ago that he was adopted. I told him my husband comes from an Island called Korkula, and the village called Velaleuca and there's Zuvelas from Blato and he said that's where his father came from. Well, I said what's his other name beside Zuvela – he said, "I don't know, what you mean?" I said all the Zuvelas I know have got hyphenated names – I don't use it – only for my pension or when I've got to use it. I said if you only knew the other part of the name I could enquire over here – I mentioned a few other Zuvelas – he said he really didn't know.

If he only knew that last name – I could have helped because there's a lot of them that come from Blato. I know that some of them live in Spearwood and some in Midland – Herne Hill. You're a Kalgoorlie-ite or a Boulder-ite whether you're a man or a woman, but they distinguish male from female where my husband comes from Valaleuca – they call him Leuchanie and they call the girls Leuschka.

I've always understood Yugoslav

I've always understood Yugoslav, I can't remember when I couldn't understand it, but I couldn't speak it, so when my husband brought one of his nephews out to the Lime Kilns, and he helped another one to come, they wanted to learn English, so they had the correspondence lessons for migrants there. This was after the war when these migrants –

they didn't get assisted by the government – these paid their own fares out. My husband brought his nephew out and my husband paid his fare. Chris would have been 23 or 24. I wrote to the University in Nedlands or somewhere – they used to send the books up and you did the lessons and posted it down and they corrected it there. Then I wrote away to Sydney for a Yugoslav dictionary – it's written by an American solicitor, and its got English and Slav and how you pronounce the English and then Slav and English, and how you pronounce it – it's written the proper way in English and then the way it's said – and by doing that I learned to speak Slav.

When I went home to Yugoslavia in 1965 and my husband said: "How did you get on?" and I said "Well nobody asked me to repeat myself – one lady in a village asked me how long since I've been home – I said I've never been here before" and apparently I speak mostly my husband's dialect. Each village, even Blato even though it's only from say Kalgoorlie to Boulder's distance away from one another – they still have a bit of a different dialect.

I used to understand everything my Mother would say in Slav, but her dialect was different than my husband's, and I used to say to her: "That's not the way". She'd say: "That's the way Mark speaks, that's the way I say it". For instance, with a needle my husband would say 'igla' and my mother would say 'yugla' – the pronunciation is a bit different and maybe spelt a bit different too.

Chapter 7
Friends, visitors and neighbours

Jean in the late 1960s, pictured with Susan Swann and Robyn Sims (facing back)

Friends, visitors and neighbours

When anyone came through it was a novelty

In the early years, we saw one couple, a husband and wife – she used to bake the bread of a night time. They were in a car, and she had a pet smoker – a parrot – and we went up because when anyone came through it was a novelty, or somebody different to speak to. And this night another lady and I went up and spoke to them and she'd made the bread, and I said: "Well, how do you do it?" She'd got that bribram and she gave me the address, I think it was King Street in Perth, because you could get it at the store and it had to be used within three months. Every night she used to bake fresh bread for the next day – she cooked it in a camp oven before they went to bed. They were camping in the open; they never had a tent, just their car.

One year, maybe 1934 or so, an autogyro landed out there for petrol and they were going to New Guinea – they said they were delivering that plane to New Guinea. That was a bit of excitement – everybody left their jobs and went down to have a look at the autogyro taxiing up to the petrol bowser. And the bloke with a name like Gansby was one of the two men in it, and they said they were going to deliver it up to New Guinea. It would have been around 1934.

And there was Jimmy Woods, the pilot, well he used to throw the paper out for us when he come over and whoever ran out and got it, read it first. Then it would be passed on. One day he threw it down with a bag of lollies – he put lollies in one of the bags that people used to use when they were airsick – he threw them down because there were two little boys there, both called Peter, but one was Aussie and one Slav. I kept the paper for years because he had written on it that this was his last trip over, because if I remember rightly … it was something to do with the

Centenary air race from London to Melbourne ... or something from England to there, and he said he was going into that air race.

He must have been going to the Eastern States from Perth ... it was like a passenger plane I think. It wasn't every day, but now and again. Once the paper was all torn, and another time it'd come down and everyone would run out, but whoever got it first would read it and passed it on.

I never saw that plane close up, but Mrs Keasey told me once that they had seen him up at Rawlinna.

That time when they had that Centenary air race, there were people that were driving over for that to Melbourne, and they came and asked us if we would have hot water and stuff if they called in. They camped at night down on a flat ... these were the people who came through in cars. In those days you went out as far as Rawlinna on the north side of the line, and from Rawlinna you went down to Cocklebiddy and that way over to the eastern States ... different to where it is there now with the Eyre Highway.

One elderly lady, we thought she was awful, because in the paper, we saw after, she said she never saw a godless and childless place, and we were really mad about that. A sea breeze came in the night she was there, and when a sea breeze comes in it blows like anything, and it blew things around where this lady and the others were. There were two children in the Kilns camp then and we had boiling water and everything for the people who were travelling. We spoke to them all right, because we were so pleased to see them – we used to love to see people there because it would break the monotony. And to say that it was a childless place, well it wasn't because these two little boys, they were the funniest kids going those two.

One of the men travelling had caught a carpet snake, or killed it, and they skinned it all and I know one of them said, "You hold the end" … to my husband, but he got a bag because he didn't like to put his hand on the skin. While the other bloke pulled the skin back, he held it with a bit on bag over the tail. Then they opened it up and nailed it on a sleeper and it was fairly wide, and this man, an Aussie boy, he kept it and got a handbag and shoes made for his wife out of it. Now, these two little boys, they were both three years of age; one was Aussie and one was Slav, and the little Aussie boy was saying … in Slav they called a snake a gooya – and the Aussie boy was saying "That's a gooya", and the Slav boy said, "It isn't, it's a snake". They were fighting about it, in opposite languages! And the Aussies and Slavs couldn't help laughing about it.

Once there were two girls, tandem bike riders, I couldn't tell you what year it was, well, those two girls, they passed through the Lime Kilns on their way over to Sydney. They had a car following, but they just stayed and rested a while and we just spoke to them and they went on. They didn't come inside – we just talked outside about what kind of a trip they had. It was the beginning of their trip; they were going east. When they came back we met them again but they only stopped a while and they said they would never do it again. It was in the Daily News of Sixty Minutes or somewhere in later years.

Another one we saw going over was Opperman. Mrs Lowe and myself were too late to get down on the flat where he rested when we found out, and he was gone before we could get close enough to speak to him, but we saw him. Hubert Opperman. When the lady tandem riders called in, they came right into the camp because the road those days was on the north side of the line. By the time he came through, the road was changed and you stayed on the south side of the line, and that's how we couldn't get down. Of course, Mrs Lowe was an older woman in her sixties and I was only twenty–four or five. When we saw them they were just ready to start again, because he'd just stopped for a spell. He was just standing beside his bike resting, but before we got there him and the chaps who were following had gone.

I've got a snap of another man who came from over east; his bike was made especially so that he could carry a fair weight on it. I'm not sure if the front wheel was smaller or not, and on it he had a little plaque hanging down from that cross bar on the bike saying where he was going. I think he was just travelling off his own bat. I was only about twenty-seven then, so it's a long while ago.

Another chap who went through on a motorbike, he said the best way to teach children geography is to go and see the places. He was a teacher in Sydney or Melbourne. He was doing this in his holidays and said he could teach the children better than by just reading it from a book. He intended to go to Europe and travel on a motorbike in the next long holidays; through Yugoslavia and that, and my husband was telling him about Yugoslavia. Anyway he went on his way – he came from the east – and the next time we heard of him was that they'd found him dead beside his motorbike. I'm not sure if it was in the Northern Territory. He got lost and yet it wasn't very far and he ran out of water – he died of thirst. I wouldn't swear to it, but I think his name was Jardine.

Harry Butler and his party called in too – they'd been out on some work – I suppose some nature thing. He had some small snakes he kept in a dampish bag, because it was cold, to keep them sleepy. The Dutch lady was living at the Kilns then – the men had killed a snake near the fowl house, and she wanted to preserve it, and she put it in a big jar with methylated spirits, and she brought it up and showed Harry Butler. He said the best way to keep them though is you've got to cut along the stomach, so that the spirit gets in, otherwise if you just put the whole snake in spirits like that it goes bad, but the other way it preserves it. They were there just for a while, and had a cup of tea. Harry Butler was

Friends, visitors and neighbours

with another chap, I can't think of his name, and Mark De Graff – he was a schoolteacher and he went out with them and also Jim Atkinson, I think he worked for Channel Seven. They were with Harry Butler. They had those little geckos – I think they must have gone out looking for those.

Vincent Serventy came out once and then his brother Dominic. They called at our place, and they must have been to Cundelee because Bob Stewart was with them. I can't tell you what year that was; it was a long time ago.

I never got to see Daisy Bates, I just heard about her, and there was a whole story of her in the *Western Mail* years ago. I never ever met her. Other people who'd seen her said that she dressed always in that old-fashioned way like Queen Victoria. But from what I can understand, they used to think a lot of her. People used to say she was very good to the blacks there.

Mr McDougall called in once to see if they could find any Aboriginals were up around that way before they dropped that bomb at Woomera. He was something with the Government. I only met them that day they called in there and they were to be sure that there were no Aboriginal people left in the area when they dropped that bomb up there. We never saw anything of the glow of the bomb, nothing at all; I suppose it was too far away. It never worried us because we were so far away from it.

He wasn't allowed on the train

Another time I met an old Aboriginal who was really well dressed, nice and clean, and he asked us ... did I see a black lady on the tea and sugar train? I said "Yes", I didn't know just what day it was and he said, "That's my wife, she's just come out of hospital", and he said, "I wasn't allowed to travel on the train". And he'd walked, and so he'd come up for a drink and then he went back and lit a fire and sat down there and I thought, poor devil, he's down there on his own. So I made a sunshine milk tin full of tea and I cut some bread and butter and jam sandwiches and I made a couple of meat sandwiches. I took it down to him, and he said, "Thanks very much lady", and he ate that.

He had come from Kalgoorlie and was going to a place called Ryan's Well … there used to be a kind of a station there. I think a chap by the name of McKenzie used to live at Ryan's Well and the Aboriginal chap was going up there. They let the wife go on the train, because she'd come out of hospital. He spoke English really well and he said: "They wouldn't let me on the train", so he walked out. My husband had to go into Naretha that afternoon and they went down and told the boss that the Aboriginal was down there, and my husband came back and said that they'd take him into Naretha. So that saved him about ten miles walk, and he only had another fourteen miles to go.

A little while after, it would have been when I was between 25 and 26, he came back, and he said: "This is for you lady". I've still got it … a meteorite, quite thick. And I said, "I don't want it", and he said, "You take it". I think that was his way of saying thank you for the meal I gave him. I took it up to Mr Moriarty at the lapidary shop to see if I could polish it, and he said: "If you polish it that takes the value off". So, he just encased it with a thin setting of silver, so that I could put on a chain and wear it.

I've also got another piece that my husband found. When he first went out he used to be fireman on the kilns, and when he wasn't firing there, sometimes he'd go out and chop wood or dig the limestone and when digging for limestone he found a couple of those meteorites.

In the early days the Aborigines used to come around, but they were no bother ... they'd never touch anything. But in later years, some of them got a bit cheeky and they'd want a drink. There was one Aussie feller and that Slav who died, and they sometimes used to give them wine, and they did have a row there once. One Aboriginal came up and said that two women are fighting down there. One bashed to the other over the head with a lump of wood, and my husband said if that was us, we'd be dead by now. Anyway, she got all right, but we had to get on to the police because one had a gun. We'd gone into Naretha, and the Slav bloke came down because he got scared. He said he wasn't going to stay up there and be killed. Anyway the brother-in-law and this Aussie fellow were standing together outside and we were just on our enclosed front verandah, and a voice called out, "Look out white man, I've got a 303" and with that, this Aussie bloke and my brother-in-law they zigzagged across the flat, and they went down and spent the night with these other people.

...and thieves

Once, when I was coming from Rawlinna, I met Mr Camilleri. I was going back to Naretha to the Lime Kilns, coming from Rawlinna in a utility, and Mr Camilleri and another chap came in their car and he asked were they very far from Rawlinna. I said no, and knowing where to look you could see the big overhead tank in the distance. And he was after somebody, I don't know whether they'd hired the car or not, or hadn't paid for it, but they were chasing the car.

Another time a chap came to the Kilns with a boy about ten or eleven and my husband said, "There's a man and a boy out there, have you got anything to give them to eat?" We'd never turn anybody away from the door and I didn't have anything much there, just the last lot of chops, because you had to wait for the tea and sugar train. My husband said, "You've got some chops, put those on". It was all the meat we had, so I out those on to fry and a couple of eggs and away that man went. And the next thing we heard (it was a midday meal I gave them) the car broke down the other side of Rawlinna, and he had to stop the train, and that car was stolen, or he was clearing out and not paying for it. They picked him up the other side of Rawlinna.

And Bill Ryan who was a ganger at Naretha, he just told us what the police had told him to tell the man to keep to the railway line, and they picked him up further along the track. We didn't see that policeman. But one night, coming through, a voice sang out, and the men said, "Oh you go out Jean, you speak English". I went out, and a chap said, "Can you tell me the road to Kalgoorlie?", and I told him and he went, and they'd been and picked up the bloke along the line, I don't know how far up. The detective went out and picked him up and he was in that car, and they were coming back to Kalgoorlie.

It might have been a month or a couple of months after, I was going into town on the passenger train. I got the train at Naretha and I got talking with this man and the man said "I was out there", and I said, "I know, you were the man who asked me the road to Kalgoorlie". He said he was one of the detectives.

Another time we had a chap at the kilns and my brother-in-law had a leather coat, and some money and when my brother-in-law came home he found some money was stolen from the camp and this leather coat was gone. We got on the pedal radio and they got on to the police, and I described the feller who took the coat and money – he was ginger-haired, freckle faced, medium height, slimly built chap, and they picked him up. He was in Kalgoorlie, and my brother-in-law only got about nine pounds of his money back, minus the leather overcoat as well. But the police got him just the same. So you have your funny moments out there.

He blew three fingers off

Life was mainly busy cooking, washing and ironing there. Sometimes before my husband was manager I used to go out bush with him a couple of times a week and just help him with the stone, and just put it in heaps instead of him stopping and picking it up. Or, when he was chopping wood I'd just put it all in a heap because the driver would come along, and stop where the heaps of wood were to load. Just to keep him company. Sometimes, I'd cook a meal and take it out to him. Instead of him taking it in the morning, I'd take it out with the driver on the second trip and go home with the first trip after lunch.

When he became boss he was just around the Kilns all the time supervising. Mostly where the men had been digging stone or chopping wood Saturdays to make a few extra bob, they used to go out all day Saturday instead of working half a day and he'd go out there in the utility he had and I always stayed home. He'd go around to where and see what they'd been doing, because with the ranger business you are supposed to leave certain trees or a certain amount and not chop it all out, and to see they were not digging out the easy stone and not leaving all the other good stone behind there.

If any blasting was done, he done the blasting, but he never used to tell me until I used to hear it go off, because when he wasn't very long in this country he went to help some friends of his, and they had never used the blasting before and he bit the fracture and was putting it in the detonator and he blew three fingers off. He only had one whole one on that hand. Another one he lost in a quarry … it got squashed when he was working in a quarry at Boya. So, he only had one whole hand. That was his own fault. When he blew them off with the blasting, he just said to his mate, "Look what I've done". They were out at Willard, past Barraclough way. His friends were out there getting wood, and the wood that they were chopping would go to the Burford soap factory at North Fremantle, and they hadn't used dynamite and fracture before so they asked my husband if he would go out and blow this wood up for him, and that's what happened. They were working for themselves, so there was no insurance.

The pedal set

We had a bad storm which cut us off for weeks, and then Mr Cranston said, we'll have to get something, a radio, a pedal set or something, and that's how we came to get that – Mr Jack Cranston was our agent at that time distributing the lime around because the Lake View and Star and those mines used to get lime for cleaning the gold there.

After the storm, some of the men got into Naretha alright and the ganger sent a telegram to Kalgoorlie for us to tell them what had happened, and tell them why the lime couldn't come in, and how the tarpaulins got burnt on the truck with the wind that lifted up the tarpaulins and the water got inside and it kind of burnt and all the trucks were just full of slack lime. Well that had to be re-bagged and everything. They bagged all that, and it got sold as slack lime.

That's when he said we'd have to get something, and they put in for a pedal radio and then we got one of those reconditioned army ones. It would have been in the war years, or maybe a bit after the war … a khaki coloured thing, and it had a lid you could take off. It was off most of the time. It was later that we got the ones of Traegar.

We had the batteries … car batteries, so we didn't have to pedal or anything. We used to charge it from the truck, take one from the other … and the same with our wireless. We had a wireless and we had to have a 6v battery, besides those big fry batteries we used to get for our wireless. We had the car battery there for the radio.

Friends, visitors and neighbours

We used it mostly when there was telegrams coming along, and in later years when Kanandah Station came along we had a bit more for one year. We used to do a lot of their telegrams, just when they were starting, and then they got their own. Eric would sometimes come in and drop a telegram and ask would I send it for him, or we'd receive some for them and we'd get our orders over the pedal radio, so really, it was darn handy.

We never had much in the line of what you'd call accidents, and the first two medical things I had on there were miscarriages, and I felt really awful. I wished it was a lady answered, not a man. This lady had a miscarriage and we called in for the doctor there. I was going into town, and my mother was there. The lady said she didn't feel well at all and her husband said to me "Will you go up and see her?" He said, "I'll take the kids out with me". He was loading stone. Anyway I went up later, and she said, "Oh I'll be alright". So she bathed herself and then I said, "Stay in bed, and I'll come up again later … just rest there." And I came up later; her husband was there and the kids were out, and she went to get up, and she just stepped out of bed, and I've never seen anything about childbirth or miscarriages before, but it just went everywhere and I wished my mother had come up. But he'd only said, would I come up, but Mum had had seven kids, and it would have been better.

But anyway, I cleaned it up and she got into bed, and I got on the pedal radio and they said for her to come into town. My husband used to come in once a month to pick up the pay and I said, "We'll come in with you". Bert, the Doctor said for her to come in right away, and we went in on the train that evening, and they had an ambulance waiting for her, and took her straight to the hospital. She was a German lady and she said that no afterbirth or nothing else came away, and they kind of wouldn't believe her until a couple of days after. She said to me, "Inside feels all cold and heavy or something", and anyway she went to the toilet and everything came away. I felt really sorry for this girl, she didn't have anybody in this country of her own.

Anyway not long after that she left, and another time one man nearly cut his big toe off, and that's about all. That time I called them and got the aerodrome, I think DCA or somewhere, and they said they were contacting the base for me, and not to worry, to stand by and everything'll be all right. And after a while they came on again and said: "Are you still there?" The chap that chopped his toe was all right though, he went on the train.

There was only twice I think the plane came out. They picked up Old Harry Dimer, he broke his leg, and he said he wasn't going to go on the plane. Well, I said, you can't be staying there, Harry." And he said: "The leg is broken." "No," I said, "Don't be silly, of course it's not". He said, "It is Jean". Anyway Dr Roberts came out himself and we had a strip that we'd made and they came out and picked Harry up.

Another time a chap, he was a dogger, was crook I think, below, kind of swollen up and he went to town as well with the plane. My husband went once, but I was away, and they took him up to Rawlinna because the plane was there. So one of the men drove him to Rawlinna and they brought him into St John of God Hospital and he'd had an infected bladder, and he was in bed for about a week before I came home. And that's about the only trouble we ever had … but it was nice to know that the plane was there, and the radio, and you got a Doctor quicker I reckon than what you do when you're living in town. They came on right away, and you can speak to the doctor, it was really good I reckon. I've talked to Dr Hansberry through the phone at the base, and within about five minutes there you've got him, whereas if you're living in town and you can't get in today, no you can come tomorrow kind of fashion. Out there you get it a darn sight quicker.

There was one old chap who had got a touch of pneumonia and we had a medical chest and they asked the age, and what nationality and all the rest and anyway, they just told us to give him these tablets, and keep him in bed, and he got alright and didn't have to come into town. So, things like that, the niece had conjunctivitis and they told us what to use there for her eyes. Even with the dogs. When the dogs got poisoned, they got on and rang Tommy Bowen at Allens there and he'd tell you what to do and it was really good. A couple of times we got on to Tom to ask about the dogs because they got poisoned.

Anything you wanted done, the operators were really good at the base. Hedley, when he was on, you'd get recipes and everything from Hedley. When he first spoke to us he said his father worked with a Zuvela, was he any relation to your husband? But his father worked in a quarry. But there was a friend of my husband, he was another Zuvela there, and he worked in a quarry, for Keasey's, they got talking about the men and had a good talk with Hedley and Lee.

We would usually end up becoming good friends with the RFDS radio operators. Lee Cordell, he was our first radio operator that I know of. We went up to his place a couple of times there and he had Christmas dinner with us one day because my brother was living up in Lyall Street in the house next door to Mrs Sharpe's two-story place. We barbecued a pig on a spit. We were at another party at his place one Christmas Eve, and she had about a dozen people there.

Kanandah gymkhanas

Kanandah station started about fourteen or fifteen miles away from us. They've got to go to Naretha to catch the train, and from there they're about eight miles from Naretha but a bit northeast I think it is, their place. We were about ten miles from Naretha if you went along the railway line. That was neighbours, and sometimes they would have pictures there and Ruth and Eric would say come in for tea and see the pictures and go home.

We were at the first gymkhana. It was really good you know, and the others then got bigger and bigger and bigger, and when it was the last gymkhana, I think there were only two of us there … Wally Scudds and me that were at the first one. Wally lives down at Norseman. I met his daughter at the Flying Doctor dinner dance … they were only little kids, and we got talking about the days when they used to be out there because he was dogging on Kanandah Station. We used to have a fabulous time. I've never been to a gymkhana since they've been up at Rawlinna. But I still don't reckon they could beat the Kanandah ones.

Everybody helped, they had someone there to do the barbecuing and that kind of business, but at first they barbecued a lamb on the spit. They'd come in with their trucks, and cars and put up their tents. They'd come in the plane … the Flying Doctor plane would be there.

Kanandah swallowed us up and they had about a mile square that was the Kiln Paddock. I told you we used to get water sent from out there from Kalgoorlie, and Kanandah, they put a bore down, about eight miles away from where we were. I think they called that 'Twenty-four', that bore, and we used to cart water from there. It was good, but there were a lot of chemicals in the water and the water was hard. When you'd do the washing, you know how you put bits if soap and powder in it, and all the scum would come up to the top, so we used to boil the water in the copper first. My husband had bought me a washing machine then, a petrol driven one, and you'd kick it over like you would a motorbike. I'd boil the water in the copper and then skim all that rubbish off, and then put it I the washing machine. Double work, but I didn't have all that rubbing and scrubbing that I used to when I first went up there.

Chapter 8

After Work

One of Jean's many pets

Lino and lights

For lights we just had tilly lamps. Old Mr Keasey had one of those lighting plants, but I'm not sure, but I think Phil Scattini took that afterwards. Mr Keasey had his refrigerator run from that plant, but it had to be done up and so we all had kero fridges. I had to get a permit for mine, because I applied for one in the war years and they said that the army came first, and when you made an application you had to put in what kind of house, and how many lived in the house and I had to wait fifteen months before I was granted a permit to get one. Eventually I got that electrolux from Mr Cranston – when things got a bit easier.

We had lino on the main floors, and sleepers on the kitchen floor; also the porch and the enclosed front verandah were sleepers. We used to buy sleepers from the Commonwealth Railways and they used them too for burning … for the kilns. They used to buy a couple of thousand and some of them that were good ones, we used them in the houses. The men adzed them so that they fitted in together in the floor. I just scrubbed them washing day with the hot water and a straw broom and I'd lift anything up that had to be up and put it on the table and then I'd throw all this boiling water from the copper all over it – you couldn't waste clean water to rinse it – and with a broom I used to go and sweep it out the back door. The rooms with lino only got washed over.

In the last years, I had lino on the bedroom floor and we called it a 'lounge room'. My husband bought a small second hand lounge, it just fitted in nicely. We had a double bed out in the front verandah as well as we only had two single beds inside. In the summer months we slept out in the enclosed verandah. In the other room I had a big kitchen, and I had my own refrigerator there.

We called the other room the 'fridge room', and we had two seven-feet cubic refrigerators in there, and I had to look after them, but that was for the men that batched. They kept their meat or beer or ice ... they were kerosene ones. They were the firm's refrigerators, but I had to have them in my place and attend to them and when the men came home from work they'd come over and get what meat they wanted, or ice etc.

I never had a row with anyone all the time we were out there. Only with the Dutch woman, once. She was a funny woman, or maybe I'm funny. We got on well with the rest of them. She must have been there a year or two ... she was a domineering kind of person, but her husband was really nice. The least said about her the better; nobody in the camp liked her. There were never any arguments.

Music to dance to

There was another building there, like a hall. We had a proper floor put into it, the company sent out the boards, and it was all filtercloth and bag all around. In the spring time when there were a lot of Sturt Peas and other flowers out, the men wouldn't let us come into the hall and they'd decorate. The women did all the cooking, old Mrs Lowe and me and the other women. I used to send into Jacksons in Collins Street in Kalgoorlie, and we used to get a fruit cake and a ham and that and the bachelors that had no wives, they'd pay for that. They'd get out a ten-gallon keg of beer and they'd sell it for sixpence a glass and what profit they made out of that, would go for the next dance. One man, I'm not sure if he was the schoolteacher, played the violin. My husband would send the truck into Naretha and bring the families that wanted to come out to the dance at the Lime Kilns. Then the following week we would all get in the truck and go to the dance at Naretha. Tommy Garner, he used to play the piano accordion and another girl and her brother could play the accordion and the schoolmaster at Naretha could play the violin ... and that was the music we had to dance to. I had a number two Metters in my place and we put the kerosene tin on that to boil the water to make coffee or tea.

So we had Saturday night dances, this week at the Lime Kilns, next week at Naretha. We had plenty of partners, because there were always more men. There were the two old Slav men who never used to bother dancing. One was one funny old chap ... he was all legs and arms, and he had a funny walk ... he went back to Yugoslavia. He was one of the two who used to look after the kerosene tin of water. This other young girl and I we said we're going to ask Old Nick and Old Mark to get up to dance. We got them up and everybody clapped, and they were laughing, because they never bothered about that kind of business. They were older than me and my husband, but anyway, they got up and jigged around and thoroughly enjoyed themselves. Everyone went to the dance; nobody stayed home, even if they didn't dance they went there because they could talk and laugh. They had their beer and what money we made out of that we'd get another keg the next week. There were only six houses in Naretha, but one family had six kids, another one had ten but a lot had grown up, and another family had nine, some still going to school. Some had left; a couple of boys were working at the kilns. We had good fun.

Jack's Mum'd sing 'On the Banks of the Wabush'

You know Jack Absalom the painter, well at that time, his father was a ganger at Naretha, and he was only a little kid, and there was another brother and sister, and he was one who used to come to the Lime Kilns. His mother, Bridget, was really nice, and she would often sing at the dance. She'd sing 'On the Banks of the Wabush'. She was really nice.

Looking back, I can't imagine Jack would be such a wonderful painter that he is. He was just a schoolkid. The mother never used to go out much at all but the father always came out, but when we went into Naretha they were always there. The little girl was the youngest, and then the tea and sugar train came into Naretha and they would go along with the wheelbarrow with the little girl sitting in it, and they used to collect Sturt Peas … the kids at Naretha did, and they'd sell to the passengers in the train. I think once Jack spoke about it on the air. People used to buy them off the kids. There were Kinnears and the Absoloms and years afterwards, his father's brother, Alec, was a ganger there at Naretha too.

When old Mrs Lowe left up there we had a party for her, and they put in and bought her a lovely leather handbag. I just don't know how much money we collected and put into, and we gave her a present of that.

Wine and water

Most of the Slavs and Italians drink, but we had half wine and water with meals. My husband said, the Aussies always put water in their whisky, whereas they should drink that straight and they drink their wine straight instead of putting water in that. They always had wine with their meals, and the men, when they were at work, they used to take, you know the flagons, they were more like the barrel-shaped flagons, rounded glass bottles, and they'd wrap paper and old flannel and a bit of bag around that and tie a bit of rope or plait up some string and make it like a handle and stitch it on to that. They'd just wet that and fill it up with water, or just about fill it, and they'd put just one glass of wine in that flagon just to break the water down, and they used to take that to work at the kilns to drink instead of the water out of the water bag. They'd fill the bottle up of a night-time and hang it out where the breeze was to cool the water down. And those that had refrigerators, their wives would have cold water, and they would put one glass of wine into the flagon and refill with cold water. Water kind of weakens you if you drink too much, and that wine usually helps them. I've heard that they did it with the water bags, but it didn't taste the same in a water bag.

I joined the library, the Mechanics Institute. Old Mr Geere, he fixed it up for me, and I used to get books in a kerosene tin. I'd keep four and send the others in, and I had that for a long time, and I had books all the time. Some people along the line, I don't know whether it was some church affair, used to send a whole pile of books down for the camps along the line. Well then when I got a lot of books I used to give them to the butcher to pass to people along the line. We didn't know them, but I don't like tearing books. Whatever books I'd had I'd pass on and others would say, "Oh, take that down to the lady at the Lime Kilns".

One year I had sixty-five Naretha Parrots

They call them Blue Bonnet, Naretha Parrot … only found around Naretha, and they've got like a blue on their head there … and a bit of yellow and orangey colour under the tail and a kind of green and tinge of bronzey on their wings. You know those weerohs, well they're about that build but they've got a long thinner tail and they haven't got a crest but this blue bonnet affair. I've had mulga parrots, but they didn't ever seem to talk. I had one for years and years, and then it went blind and died.

One year I had sixty-five Naretha Parrots there and I was up all hours of the night. My husband wouldn't bother about them. I used to feed them. There was a lady who wanted a Naretha parrot and apparently she met my brother Jack, and she must have been talking about parrots, and Jack gave her my name and address; she lives in

Chatswood NSW. We used to get them from the nests, and I had sent some to SA before, but I had to write away to the wildlife, fisheries or something like that and get a permit and then get this license. And then when you sent the birds over east you had to give the license to the guard on the train. Anyway, this time I wrote and asked for the license to be able to send some over and when I asked for this permit they said no, that the birds were protected now and I'd have to let them all go.

I couldn't let them go. I gave them away to different people. I kept a pair for quite a while, but this man Mr Gillespie, who used to be Mayor of Boulder … I don't know how he knew my or my husband's name but a friend of Mr Gillespie's sent this man to my place and he came up to my place in Addis Street, and he said he had a permit from the government to breed these birds. He said, "I've got Naretha parrots but they are getting too in-bred", and he wanted to know would I sell these two of mine. And I didn't like to, because the male was beginning to talk and I thought to myself, my husband would say, "Gee you're mad, what's the use of keeping them", and anyway I sold them to him.

I had five dogs and three cats … some of the dogs went bush in the finish. I think they must have mated up with dingoes, and two other I had, I think somebody in the camp must have poisoned them. My sister-in-law said she saw them when she was up at midnight, but in the morning one of them was dead and the other died not long afterwards. The other one had a bit of dingo in it … he lost a leg … got caught in a dingo trap and this Mr Scudds found it after a couple of days and they had to cut the leg off because it was only hanging by a sinew. The leg healed up just as if a vet had done it. That dog had never bitten anybody but everybody wouldn't understand … he'd come along and smell you and then take no notice, but he had a bad habit of running after cars and I got Eric Swann to shoot it for me.

Chapter 9
The Kilns close

Jean and Mark celebrate their Golden Wedding Anniversary in 1982

And then I howled because I was leaving

When I went to the Lime Kilns, I was twenty-three, and the years just went by. I'd done one year away from there on the Kurrawang Woodline, and I went into Kalgoorlie from out there when I was 57, and then I howled because I was leaving. That was the only home I'd had.

We came into Kalgoorlie on the 5th January 1966 because they closed the Kilns down. It cost too much and they put that lime-burning thing there that they've got now at Parkeston. They took me out to see it. I said that if my husband was alive he'd tell you that that lime is not as good as the lime we burnt at the Lime Kilns out there. And when I saw it, it was an aluminium sort of colour. I said the lime we burnt out there was white. Well it had to go through another process to become white. It only needs a couple of blokes to work there at Parkeston, but they've got limestone from around Kitchener somewhere, around the 950 mile, and there's like grit in it or shell, and that would be about thirty or forty miles west of the Lime Kilns there. I think that was under the ocean once because in amongst that stuff there's a lot of shells of all sizes and shapes. Well, that is real solid stone … proper limestone. And my husband said to me, it's just like the limestone they got in the old country where he lived, because they've got limestone, but they burnt it a different way over there.

They learnt to treat lime in the old country. Then he saw how Charlie Keasey built, and a lot of them where my husband comes from do stone masonry work, they never went to school to learn, it was just part of their upbringing like.

When we left, all the buildings were sold to Cundelee native mission but they weren't where they are now at Coonana; they were in the old place. It's not far from Zanthus ... I don't know how far. They bought the iron and the tanks and the stoves ... most of the houses where the women were living had stoves. Also some people left wardrobes and iron bedsteads, and we just told the Cundelelee people to take those. All that's left there is just the Lime Kilns.

I gave my white-topped table to people further on, another station, Gunnadorah, to Rosary Day. I brought the kitchenette that the lady paid seven pounds ten for – I brought that into town. My home-made table got left. But the rest of the stuff – I had a lounge – we gave them to somebody who took them away.

I brought those two Naretha Parrots and another dog into Kalgoorlie. He got hit by a car and went blind. He wasn't in pain and could find his way all around the house. And one day I said to my husband, "Where's the dog, Rexie?" And we looked but never found him from that day to this.

They closed the Kilns down on the 5 December 1965, and we were the last ones to come in to Kalgoorlie. My husband didn't do any work for a while, but then he got a job on the Lake View and Star, through Jack Barker, who was our agent after Cranston gave it up and he got a job for Mark out there. He used to clean the offices and do some gardening around the place, until he left off work when he was seventy-two. He got the flu very bad and he said to me: "I just feel Jean, that I can't go back to work no more", and so he gave up working altogether.

I got a job with Mrs Scott at the Australia Guest House. I just did the bedrooms downstairs and upstairs. I was there for a little over two years. Then I went for a trip to Fiji and then I came back and went and worked at the Big K Laundromat for over four years. Then I worked at the Vienna Coffee Lounge for quite a while, but I didn't work full-time.

Mary used to take me to the hospital to see Mum...

Mum died in a home around in Mt Lawley when she was 83. She died on the 19th June and would have been 84 on the 10th December 1972.

She was living with my sister when she got bad, and my sister couldn't manage – old age, and the arteries of the heart were hardening as well. She must have had a slight stroke which affected her head and her mind went back. We used to go and see her when I came down from Kalgoorlie – I used to catch the day train. I arrived in the afternoon and went straight from there. Mary used to take me to the hospital to see Mum before we went home to my sister's.

Mum kind of knew us. She would get up and I'd say: "Where are you going Mum?" She said "Oh to put some wood on the fire". I said "Oh, that's alright, I put the wood on the fire as I came along there". She said: "I don't know if the boys have anything for tea". I said "Oh, there's plenty there, don't worry". Her mind had gone back and I think she thought the boys were coming from work.

In the finish she never spoke at all, she just looked at you, and it was an effort to keep on talking. But every time I got there, I used to get a dread because it was my mother, and it wasn't my mother. She wasn't like that – she was so fussy with herself, and she got in such a way … well, she used to wet herself. She didn't know and she'd wet the bed and I know we got there one day and she was pulling the sheets. I think it was uncomfortable and they'd have to tie her in the bed. To sit her up they used to tie her in the chair – at least she'd sit up straight like that.

They looked after her really well. The doctor said about two years, and it was. It would have been two years in the November. She was sitting in a chair and Mary was talking to her – they dress you up you know. She was sitting near a window so that she could see outside. They ran out after Mary, but she'd gone, and by the time she got home it was about three quarters of an hour. They rang Mary and said that: "Our dear friend, our favourite patient – she's just passed away. We ran out after you but you'd gone". And Mary said; "You know Jean, how Mum was always fiddling around" – not like me, she was very fussy and Mary's taken after her. Everything's got a place, and everything's in its place ... and she'd never sit and do nothing. One day she was fiddling, and I said: "what are you doing Mum?" and she said, "Oh, I'm just mending", and her fingers were always moving. And Mary said, "You know, now when I look back Jean, Mum's hands were still. She must have died while I was there, when I walked out". Mary, she always turned at the door and said to Mum "Oh, I'll see you tomorrow" ... though she never used to talk.

The nurses said she used to talk, she used to talk about me, but she never used to say anything to me there, or to Mary. We'd stay there for half and hour or so, and talking to her all the time and not a word. She'd just look at you all the time, and one of the nurses said to Mary: "She talks about you". Once, one of the nurses said to my mother "Your daughter's coming down, do you know who she is?" And she said: "Yes, she's mine". But to Mary and I she would just sit there and look at us, and her hands were always plucking at something.

So I went to Perth

And then in 1982 my husband died, so I went down to Perth. There was only just him and I. I didn't work in Perth, that was the worst part of it ... if I could have got a job it would have got me out of the place, but sitting there all day with nothing to do, no gardening, I didn't like it. There was only me, so the place never got dirty. That's when I felt I wished I had a car, and could drive. I'd never learnt to drive. My sister has got a car and she just hops in it and goes here there and everywhere. She used to go dressmaking and was always having people coming in and out.

I'd gone into Boans one day to do some shopping and the most awful feeling came over me. It seemed that everything was coming down on the top of my head, the people going this was and that way, I just felt as if something was coming down. I said, "Get out of this Jean!", and I went straight out into St George's Terrace and got a bus and came home. What I was going to do at Boans, I don't know from that day to this. All I did was turn around and went straight out into St George's Terrace. It only happened that once – it was just like claustrophobia. I had been shopping before and never had that feeling before or since, but that day I did.

Perth's not like it was years ago. I used to love going down to Fremantle. When I stepped on that train, I'd think: "I'm home", because I like Fremantle. When I used to come down from the bush, well the day before I was ready to go back to the bush again I used to go to Perth on my own and I'd go here there and everywhere, to the places and shops that I liked. I'd say, "God knows when I'll be down again to see you", and then go back to the bush.

But that day, I don't know, I felt awful. I said: "Blow this, I'm going back to Kalgoorlie". As luck happens, I hadn't had a chance to sell my house, so I came back. I also went back to my old job at the Vienna Coffee lounge. A bit later, I shifted in not far from Heather Crombie's place there because up in Addis street was a quarter acre block – too many fruit trees, roses and vines in the garden. I couldn't keep it going like my husband did, so I got a smaller block with not much garden but a lawn at the front and back and I could easily keep it tidy, and the house was smaller.

I'd always wanted to go to the Two-up

I always liked to have a bet on the horses – we would have a bit of a bet when we played cards at Kurrawang and I always enjoyed having a bit of a flutter. The men from the kilns would go out to the Two-up when they went to Kalgoorlie – it was out in the bush a bit out of town there, on the Leonora road, and they would have a bet; it was really popular in those days. But no women were allowed out there and then they changed that rule after I went to Kalgoorlie and I always wanted to go and have a bet out there. Heather Crombie had won some money out at the races, it must have been around Race Round time and she said "Let's go out to the Two-up". She had been to the races with Bob Crombie and he told her not to put the money on this horse but she did and she won there, so we went out to the Two-up.

There's two rings out there, one's for the really big gamblers. And this fellow, one of the McMeikan boys, came up to as and said "What are you ladies doing here?' because even though women were allowed out there now not many went because it was mostly men. So he told us not to go to that big ring because that was where all the big gamblers went, and he said he would put a bet on for us in the other ring, and we had a few bets and won some.

But afterwards we wanted to have a look at the big ring so we went over there just to look and there was that Mrs Wong from the Chinese Restaurant there, the one in St Barbara's square. She was a large woman there and had this carpetbag that she kept all her money in; and she had money in the pockets of her smock as well and she was one of the bigger gamblers, there would have been about fifteen of them and the rest were just watching – it was pretty crowded. The Two-up was really popular in those days, not like now; it's sort of died off since they started doing

Two-up at the races. But in those days they even took the tourist buses out there.

So we were watching and there were quite a lot of Slavs out there but I didn't know any of them – they were talking in Slav and telling each other what to do. There were two blokes near us and they must have thought that we wouldn't be able to understand them because they started talking about that Mrs Wong in Slav and they weren't being very nice and I was getting uncomfortable because I could understand what they were saying. So, then I turned around and talked back to them in Slav and told them that what they were saying wasn't nice, but I used some words that they were using and the shock on their faces! Well, we went home after that and we were laughing all the way back to Kalgoorlie, but I wouldn't tell Heather what I said because it wasn't really nice there and I just said it to shock them, and it did! Laugh – I can still see the looks on their faces.

Jack had that asbestosis

I went back down to Perth about five times on account of my older brother near the end. Apparently he had that asbestosis for a while before we knew and he knew he had a shadow on his lung. We were down at his place for New Year, but he wouldn't let us know. I said: "Where did you get it, you never worked at Wittenoom". He said: "On the wharf, handling it". He was a lumper on the wharf. His mates ... some of them from the wharf died. He lasted out the longest – he never smoked and wasn't a heavy drinker. The specialist said it was only that he was physically fit that he lasted as long as he did.

They took fluid off his lungs as well, and he was in and out of hospital. He wasn't married, but he had a defacto wife, and his own wife couldn't have done any more than what she did. She was really good to him. In the finish he died in the Sir Charles Gardiner hospital. They did tell him once they had a breakthrough but nothing that would help him. They had an autopsy on him – she didn't like the idea, but the son said yes. The oldest son was in Adelaide, and the second oldest was in charge, next of kin, and he said well maybe they might find something to help somebody else. The worst type of asbestosis you could get, he got it.

We missed the older brother after he died. I had the young brother up and he said: "Jean, I've been beginning to miss Jack now, more than I did at first". He'd heard a Kombi van – Jack had a kombi van – and it pulled up across the road, and he said: "Oh God, there's Jack coming". You know, for a second I expected him.

I had stayed up at Kalgoorlie and was kind of out of it, away from my family, as all my other brothers and sister were down Perth way. Jack had been in East Fremantle, sister Mary is in Como; Frank is in a war service home at Mt Lawley. But living near the Crombies – they lived at 75 and the Clews were in the middle of us – Heather is really good to me and I was like a part of their family too. And the Swanns, even when they were still out at Kanandah, they would stay with us when were still up in Addis Street there, and after, when I moved down to Varden Street they still visited. Heather would drive me to the doctor and places, but I still like to walk – I always liked walking. I used to walk from our camp into the main camp at Kurrawang, and at the Lime Kilns, I was always walking there. But it's not always so easy now and Heather drives me.

I sometime wish I was closer to Perth there where my two brothers and sisters are. I can go down and visit, but you go down and it just seems to run away with money.

Eulogy for Jean
By Eric Swann

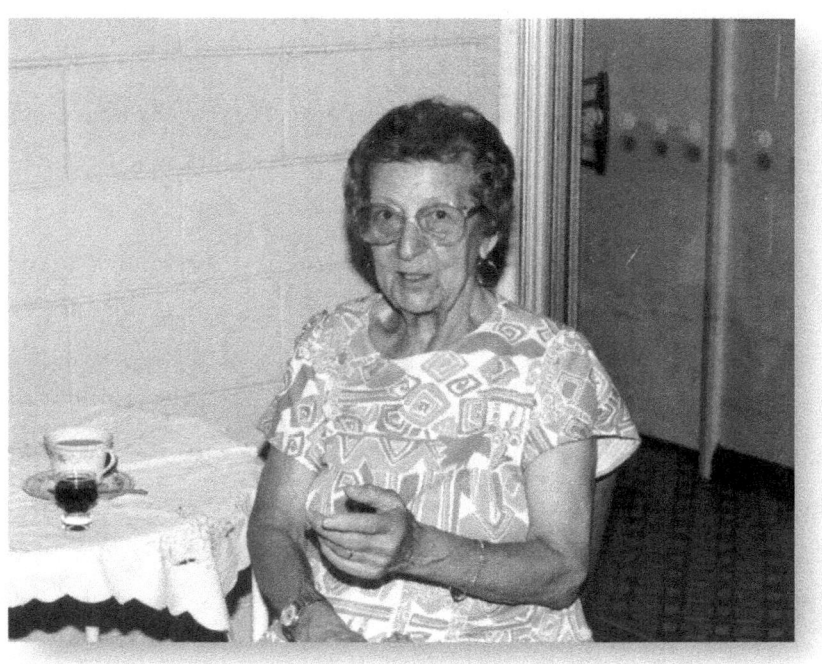

I was flown to the Nullarbor in December 1962 to have a look at my new job. This was to develop the country which was to be known as Kananadah station. We were met at the airstrip near the Lime Kilns by Mark Zuvela. We were then taken to their home where we met Jean and were treated to some of her wonderful cooking. This was to be the first of many meals.

It was also the start of my family's involvement with the Nullarbor Plain, but more importantly it was the commencement of a wonderful friendship with Mark and Jean.

Jean Strika arrived at the Lime Kilns in 1933. She was aged 24 and had come to be the cook and housekeeper for her two brothers, Frank and Jack, and two other men, one of whom was Mark who became her husband the following year.

The Kilns, on the Western edge of the Nullarbor Plain were to be Jean's home for 33 years – apart from one year which she and Mark spent on the wood lines.

Jean became the complete bush woman, and the 'Lady from the Lime Kilns' became known across the Nullarbor and indeed many miles beyond. Mark and Jean's generosity was extraordinary. No traveller passed the Kilns without being properly fed and watered, and treated to the warm hospitality always shown to everyone. Surely these people were Christians in the true sense of the word.

Speaking of Christianity, I recall being at Mass at the Kilns one morning when a travelling priest came through. I was impressed by an almost 100% attendance by the kiln population, I found out later that Mark gave the crew the option of attending Mass or continuing work on the Kilns, and work they did, as Mark stood at the door of the house while Mass was on and made sure they did keep working.

By Eric Swann

During those first few months before Ruth and our kids arrived at the station, and I was camped just out from the Kilns, Jean and Mark were wonderful help. Mark organised unloading material from railway trucks when I was short of time and Jean sent and received reams of telegrams through RFDS, which was our only form of communications at the time. Also, if I came through late there was always a cooked meal ready in the oven.

Jean took the young fellows who were working for me under her wing too. She looked after their good clothes, fitted them out dressed in the best available from each suitcase when they caught they train to Kalgoorlie. When they returned she washed and ironed the clothes and returned them to the right case.

Mark and Jean did not have children of their own but they adopted ours into their family when Ruth and our four arrived from Adelaide. Later, when Heather and David Sims arrived, their children were included Jean and Mark's expanded family. Indeed Mark and Jean became Uncle and Aunt to half the kids on the Nullarbor. Jean's favourite saying was "Come on shrimp (or sausage) take no notice of your mother, have more cake, you're in my house now".

The Kilns closed at the end of 1966 and Jean and Mark moved to Kalgoorlie. Their new home became home away from home for the Swanns and the Sims for some years.

As you would all know, Jean was quite a talker. Many an appointment I had was late because I couldn't get a word in to say I had to go. Jean liked talking about people and places – particularly her family. I feel I knew all of Jean's family, even though there were some that I never met. Her talk was never malicious or critical. She liked people, and she loved kids.

After Mark's death in 1982, Jean moved to a house in Varden

Street, almost next door to Heather and Barry Crombie. Ruth and Heather had adopted Jean as their surrogate mother and this bond strengthened over the years. In particular, Heather's devotion to Jean's welfare in her later years earned a huge debt of gratitude from all of us who loved Jean.

Needless to say, Jean's band of friends grew when she moved to Kalgoorlie. She was a vigorously active woman both physically and mentally throughout her life, even well into her later years. People remarked that she still walked like a young girl when she was into her late 70's. Even though her body started to fail she was mentally alert until the very end.

We will all miss her terribly, but she has now gone to join her beloved Mark, and who would deny her that final goal. She loved her families dearly, both her blood family and her adopted family. She was proud of the achievements of all, particularly the young ones. Jean was one of a very special breed, many of whom pass unsung into history. She was a pioneer bushman and to me that is the highest endorsement.

In closing may I say with absolute sincerity and humility…. "Thank you Jean from us all for the years you spent with us and may you rest in peace."

About the Author

Born in the 1950s, Jenny Kroonstuiver spent her childhood living on pastoral stations firstly in western Queensland and then on the Nullarbor Plain in Western Australia. It was during the time on the Nullarbor that she met Jean and Mark Zuvela, who became life-long adopted 'Aunt and Uncle'.

Jenny trained as a teacher and spent several years teaching in country areas of the Northern Territory and Queensland, before returning to Kalgoorlie in the 1980s. After a short-lived marriage, she raised her four children alone, continuing to work in the broader education sector. From 2004, she took up a role managing the national training system for the Australian meat industry, a role she held until her retirement in 2020.

www.ingramcontent.com/pod-product-compliance
Lightning Source LLC
LaVergne TN
LVHW011846060526
838200LV00054B/4195